What to Do When He Won't Change

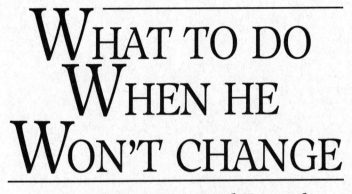

WHAT TO DO WHEN HE WON'T CHANGE

Getting What You Need From the
Man You Love

DR. DAN KILEY

G. P. PUTNAM'S SONS / NEW YORK

G. P. Putnam's Sons
Publishers Since 1838
200 Madison Avenue
New York, NY 10016

Library of Congress Cataloging-in-Publication Data

Kiley, Dan.
What to do when he won't change.

1. Men—United States—Psychology. 2. Men—United
States—Attitudes. 3. Interpersonal relations.
I. Title.
HQ1090.3.K545   1987   646.7′8   87–6053
ISBN 0–399–13324–0

Printed in the United States of America
1 2 3 4 5 6 7 8 9 10

CONTENTS

*Grant me the knowledge to change
the things that I can change,
the serenity to accept
the things I cannot change,
and the wisdom to tell the difference.*

INTRODUCTION:
WHY LOVING
CONFRONTATION
IS THE ONLY WAY

"I'm willing to do anything to make this relationship work," Julie said. "I only wish Andy could say the same. But he insists he's not doing anything wrong. He says that if I'd just quit worrying, we'd be fine."

Julie is a 38-year-old woman with a tired and drawn look on her otherwise attractive face. She is married to a 42-year-old professional named Andy, who says he loves her but who never shows it. Julie loves Andy and she doesn't want a divorce, but every time she takes steps to improve their relationship, Andy either criticizes or ignores her. Hers is a no-win situation.

Despite all her efforts, Julie still blames herself for the failures in her relationship. "I'll tell you how bad my guilt is, Dr. Kiley," she said. "I'm so relieved I was busy the whole day of the Chernobyl nuclear accident; that way, I know for sure I didn't cause it."

The sadness in Julie's eyes as she spoke hinted that she had exaggerated, rather than fabricated, her guilt. It was a by-product of her misguided notion that she could *make* Andy change—if only she could find the right combination to unlock his feelings for her. Because she can't, her self-esteem has begun a dangerous plunge toward depression. But although she was at the end of her rope when I saw her, she and I both knew that she was far from quitting.

"Tell me how things sank so low," I gently asked this young woman, who already looked middle-aged.

Julie tried to smile through the tears that welled up in her eyes. "I fell off the edge again last Sunday. I promised myself it would never happen again."

"What do you mean, 'fell off the edge'?"

"Actually, it started Saturday. Andy and I had a lot of errands to do, and all day long he was either critical of everything I said or else he acted as if I wasn't even there. I knew he was feeling bad, but I didn't know why. When he gets that way, I'm very careful not to say or do the wrong thing."

Her eyes flooded with tears so I rose to turn off the overhead fluorescent lights to reduce the glare. "Thank you," she said softly and then began to cry quietly. "I can't do anything right. I can't organize my house, my job, or my kids. I can't control my moods. My relationship with Andy is slipping away from me, and every time I try to do something to stop it, it only makes matters worse."

"Let's go back to 'falling off the edge,' " I said.

She nodded. "We had to make a decision about what kind of wallpaper to put up in the kitchen. We'd already taken the old wallpaper down, and it had been looking terrible for six months. Andy kept saying that he'd investigate the best buy, but that's all he did—investigate. So finally I said, 'Honey, you've been checking out wallpaper for six months; isn't it time we just bought something?' Well, he turned quiet and wouldn't talk, and I realized I had hurt him. We went to a party that night, and I tried to have fun in spite of the fact that he was punishing me by talking to everyone except me.

"I woke up Sunday morning determined to have a good day and get the house organized. At about ten in the morning I was standing in the kitchen when Andy came in and asked me if I'd like to go back to bed and have sex. Sex with Andy has been on again, off again recently, and I thought lovemaking might help us get back on track, so I said, 'Sure!'

"I guess I should back up and tell you that when we were first married, Andy and I had fabulous sex. But over the past few years it's become mechanical. He won't hold my hand or kiss me unless we're in bed. I've tried to talk to him about being more romantic without coming right out and criticizing him. I have to be very careful not to hurt him or scare him off. I've said things like, 'Think of how you used to like watching our bodies together, and all those sexy thoughts we used to share.' Even a year ago he would have taken this the wrong way, but he trusts me more now—as long as I'm very careful.

"So, anyway, I suggested that we take a shower together, but he said he didn't want to. Well, to make a long story short, it didn't work."

"Meaning he couldn't keep an erection?" I asked.

"Yes."

"Then what happened?"

"Oh, I tried to put on a happy face and went out to the kitchen to make Andy some hot chocolate. And that's when I fell off the edge."

"Tell me exactly what happened," I said gently.

"As I stood at the sink I had this growing feeling of indecisiveness. I began thinking of everything I had to do, how I was wasting too much time. I thought I should do one thing, but when I started to do it, I stopped and said 'no,' and then went in another direction.

"I kept trying to tell myself to pray, to calm down, but I tried and it didn't work. I remember thinking, 'I should be able to use some technique to straighten myself out.'

"That's when Andy came into the kitchen and said, 'We're not romantic anymore.' Immediately this horrible rage began building up inside me. 'No,' I said, '*you're* not romantic anymore; it's not me!' I think I was screaming. He turned and walked away."

"Then what did you do?"

"Well," she said softly, "for a minute I felt great. Then I felt even worse. On the outside I was proud of myself for speaking out, but on the inside I was damning myself for being so bitter toward Andy. I realized I had overreacted, that I'd hurt him,

13

and I knew he wouldn't talk to me again for a long time. For the next hour I started raging all over the house."

"What do you mean by 'raging'?" I asked.

"I would wander from room to room doing nothing, then sit down and cry like a baby, then scream out loud that I was sick and tired of going nowhere with our relationship and having no help. Then I would sit quietly, and it would start all over again."

"And is this what you mean by 'falling off the edge'?" I asked gently.

She nodded.

"What did Andy do while you were raging?"

"Went down to the family room and watched football," she answered matter-of-factly.

I shook my head in disbelief. "You know, don't you, that this whole thing is ridiculous?"

"Tell me about it!" she said bitterly.

"Obviously what you're doing is not working," I said, "but are you ready to try something else?"

"What other choice do I have?" Julie said. "I want my sanity back."

You Can't Make Him Change

Julie is married to a man who won't change. Although she tries her best to make him love her, nothing seems to work. Her efforts only bring derision, which in turn makes her feel *she* is the one who is at fault; and this is the cause of her overall sense of guilt. She is a bright, caring woman, but she feels foolish for loving Andy so much, especially when he is so cruel to her in return. Something has to give.

There are many women like Julie who ask, "What can I do if he won't change?" However, most situations, are a little less extreme (at least, I hope so). In order for you to find help in this book, it is not necessary that your man be as resistant to change as Andy was. In fact, if he is basically good-hearted but won't change in one or two areas, then this book can offer you almost immediate relief.

If you are one of the thousands of women who are in love

with a man who won't change, chances are your man does one or more of the following: he dumps his frustrations on you; he is indifferent to your concerns; he still believes that women like "macho" men; he isn't there when you need him; he refuses to admit his mistakes; he takes you and your love for granted; and he won't often share his feelings.

I am not suggesting that you try for a "perfect" man or a "perfect" marriage. Only that you should expect to have a man who will control his temper, show concern for your problems, share his weaknesses with you, put loving you ahead of filling up his own ego or pocketbook, and, most of all, be there when you need him. In other words, you deserve a man who can *demonstrate* his love by his behavior.

When I've asked women why they don't leave a man who won't change, almost all of them have admitted that they've thought of leaving him but have stopped themselves for various reasons. They may want to try and recapture the wonderful times they used to have; they may be financially unable to leave; they may believe that life after divorce would not be that much better; or—and this is the reason I hear most often—they know that their man really wants to love them, and they're bound and determined *to make him change*.

But it never works. It never has and it never will. Under normal circumstances, one person—no matter how powerful he or she might be—cannot force another to change his basic view of life. The only possible exception to this is the brainwashing process to which prisoners of war and members of certain cults are subjected. Apparently, controlling a person's immediate environment—light, food, sleep, and human contact—can wear down his drive for self-determination and force him to change his fundamental way of dealing with society. But even then, follow-up studies indicate that his self-determination will return if the harsh controls over him are lifted.

So although you may be able to intimidate your man into saying the right words, down deep you know that it won't last. He won't change the way he *thinks*, and, given half a chance, he'll make you pay for your intimidation.

Consider this far-from-perfect analogy: imagine, for a moment,

15

that your relationship with your man is a game of cards. The cards each of you has in your hand are dealt according to individual genetic inheritance and the impact of early childhood. (Experts say that the first five to seven years are most crucial.) Although we have little control over the cards we're dealt, we *can* control how we choose to play them.

When you try to make him change, you are, in effect, leaning across the table, taking him by the hand, and forcing him to play a certain card. You yourself know how you'd react if someone tried to do that to you—you'd rebel. So does he.

When their frustration reaches a breaking point, many women unwittingly sink into the trap of thinking that they somehow control the cards their man holds. Julie had fallen into that trap. Her self-esteem had hit such a low point, that she had begun to think that she somehow caused Andy to treat her the way he did. In a state of mild depression and panic, she convinced herself that she had dealt him his hand and thus tried to redeal him different, more effective cards.

What *do* you do when he won't change? You play your cards in the most rational, well-planned way you can and hope that your man will *choose* to change the way he plays his cards. Your actions become a catalyst for change. In other words, you stimulate change but are not the cause of it.

You do this by using your verbal and nonverbal behavior to confront him and the way he plays his cards toward you. You trump or ignore the cards you don't want; you play the cards you want him to play, hoping he gets the idea; you change the frequency or the type of the cards you play; you give him information about card playing; sometimes you refuse to play; and, most importantly, no matter what strategy you employ, you play your cards in a loving, supportive manner. That way there's no regrets and no room for guilt if he chooses to consistently play his uncaring and inconsiderate cards and you choose to quit playing with him.

When you control your actions in the most rational and well-planned manner possible, with the purpose of influencing your man's behavior, you are in effect answering the question, What can I do if he won't change?

16

I taught Julie how to confront Andy in a loving way. She learned attitudes and actions that would give her a realistic chance of improving her marriage. Most of the programs she learned were actual behavioral prescriptions detailing the "how," "what," "when," and "where" of such techniques as sharing information, demonstrating skills of conflict resolution, explaining problem-solving methods, avoiding damaging interactions, and, in certain situations, directly confronting her man's disrespectful behavior.

Making a decision about what to do if your man won't change isn't as difficult as you might think. In fact, you will be reminded several times that one of the most powerful actions you can take is explaining your behavior to your man after he recognizes that something in you has changed and asks, "What's going on here?"

This book will first teach you how to overcome certain obstacles in yourself. Then it will show you how to use your new found strength and self-control to implement techniques that *may* act as catalysts to change the behavior of your man.

At the end of my first session with Julie, I gave her a homework assignment. She was to practice programs that would help her achieve self-acceptance, control of bitterness, and the development of an internal locus of control. I knew from research and from my clinical practice that these programs would provide her with immediate relief and a feeling of long-term personal stability. But just as importantly, she would also be learning an overall method of loving confrontation that would give her relationship its best chance of survival.

Self-Management Psychology

Ten years ago I would have taken a much different approach with Julie. I would have guided her through a labyrinth of trial-and-error exercises, continually assuring her that she would eventually find solutions to her problems. It was an approach that often worked, but not nearly often enough and certainly not fast enough. Too many women drop out of therapy because the last thing they need is another long-term stress to endure.

Now I felt no hesitancy in giving Julie behavioral prescriptions for immediate implementation. I was confident because I had

undergone a professional transition from traditional psychother-
apy, in which the therapist is in charge of the session, to a new
psychology—the psychology of self-management—in which the
therapist acts as a teacher, offering problem-solving methods to
the patient, who is seen as a student. Self-management psychology maintains that the patient, or student, is his or her own
best therapist.

"Can you give me an example?" Julie asked me, when I first
told her about loving confrontation.

"Sure. Many women complain that their man won't share his
feelings. 'I know he feels terrible,' they may say, 'but he won't
talk about it.' So they feel cheated and rejected. One of my
programs of loving confrontation shows women how to teach their
partner to replace 'feelings' with 'internal reactions.' It says the
same thing: feelings are internal states of arousal; but it says it
in a nonthreatening way that encourages learning."

Julie's face clouded with bitterness. "Oh, we mustn't threaten
the little boys, must we?"

"Naturally you feel bitter," I said. "But I think loving confrontation can help you with that, too. Let me show you how. You've
said Andy is insensitive and that he won't change, right?"

"Yes."

"And, you've concluded that he doesn't really care about your
feelings."

"Well," she said slowly, "that might be a little strong."

"I want you to use a program called *relabeling* and think that
Andy doesn't express his sensitivity or work with you to solve
your problems *because he doesn't know how.* How does that thought
feel?"

"Oh," she said tentatively, "it makes me feel sorry for him,
I guess."

"But you must know," I said, "that neither extreme—bitterness or pity—will help the two of you. The purpose of relabeling
is to put a new perspective on an old problem in order to give
yourself a way out of it.

"So where is this new perspective supposed to lead me?" Julie
asked.

"Into the role of *teacher.* Whether or not he'll admit it, today's man needs a woman's help—not her salvation or pity—her help. He needs her to teach him how to be a sensitive human being in a highly interpersonal world, something she's been doing a hell of a lot longer than he has.

"Today's man is in trouble. He pretends to be competent, but in truth he faces a world fraught with pressure. He lacks the inner resources to cope with it. He really wants to love his woman, but too often he simply doesn't know how. His stance is that of hunter and protector, but women don't need him in that role anymore. Most women want their man to be a mental companion, to help them deal with the issues of belonging and self-esteem.

"Granted, women also are going through a tough time. But they are still in far better shape than men. Women have the ability to open up to friends about their fears and insecurities. Men are stuck inside an obsolete 'macho' image, wondering how the hell they got that way and pretty much convinced that there's no way out."

I leaned forward, took Julie's hand, and looked into her eyes. "We men need your help. So give us your best shot, and if we still don't wake up and realize what we're missing, *then* walk away. But don't condemn us for being blind. Turn on the light, and we might see the truth."

Learning to Teach

Insurance industry statistics suggest that a warm, loving relationship can add up to nine years to a man's life. That's because a loving relationship can help a man learn to identify his feelings, share them, and solve those problems that generate them. Men want those additional nine years, and they need a woman's help to get them.

You can help add years to your man's life, and life to both your years. But first you have to become an expert teacher. This book is your guide. To make it work for you, you must achieve two goals. First, you must *prepare yourself* (Part I) to become the most competent teacher you can be. Then, you must *confront him lovingly* (Part II) and encourage him to learn from you. If

19

your loving confrontation is successful, be prepared for the student eventually to outshine the teacher in some areas. Then the teacher can begin learning from the pupil.

Throughout this process, keep in mind that the student always has the right to refuse the lessons the teacher offers. Hence, even when you've become the best teacher you can possibly be, you still are not completely responsible for the student's learning.

"I think you're getting the wrong picture of Andy," Julie said toward the end of our second session. "He can be a loving and kind man, and I want to stay with him. I just have to find another way to handle myself when we have problems. What I'm doing now is only making things worse, and I end up hating myself more. I want my marriage to work, and I'll do whatever it takes to make it happen."

"Even if it leads you to the realization that your marriage isn't going to work?" I asked.

"I'll only give up," Julie said, "after I've given it my best shot and it still hasn't worked. And up to this point, I really haven't given it my best shot."

"Then," I said, not hiding my admiration of her courage, "you've come to the right place."

1.

ARE YOU READY FOR
CHANGE?
TWO QUIZZES

The Wisdom Quiz

Before preparing yourself or confronting him, you should be able to answer the question, What am I trying to achieve? Chances are you've been running around in circles, saying one thing and doing another. Your behavior has no consistency. In other words, you haven't had a goal. You've succeeded only in proving to your man that your request for sensitivity and intimacy is just one more thing he can ignore.

Below you will find a two-part quiz for establishing personal goals—yours and his. Each part contains a list of ten traits that the latest psychological research indicates are vital to both partners for a lasting love relationship.

Quiz yourself as to the degree to which each trait is present in either you or your partner by using a scoring of 0 = never; 1 = sometimes; 2 = always.

HE:

He Spends Some Time Alone.

Silence, and the mental "idling" that accompanies it, are essential for coping with stress and understanding one's inner world. To profit from silence, a man must balance his drive to be active and involved with moments where he does nothing. Sitting in a chair meditating or taking a solitary walk will help your man know himself, and gain strength from that knowledge.

He Controls His Competitiveness.

When he plays games (e.g., Scrabble, tennis, cards), is he able to laugh at himself, to avoid drawing attention to himself excessively, and to accept defeat somewhat graciously? Competitiveness is healthy provided that it is *intra*personal. This means that a man should compete with and try to improve upon his own past performances, not the current performance of another.

He Understands His Relationship with His Father.

A man's relationship with his mother has been overemphasized to the exclusion of his relationship with his father. To be a good love partner, a man must have an understanding of his relationship with his father, or, if not, be able to talk about any sadness he feels without self-pity or hostility. A man who has experienced his father as loving and vulnerable, yet strong, is likely to be a wonderful lover.

He Has Empathy for You.

Is he able to predict how you will feel when you are in an emotional situation? To have empathy for you requires that a man be able to place his own ego on the back burner and turn his attention to your experience. He must be able to listen, understand, ask questions, and restate your words in such a way as to approximate your experience. Empathy is absolutely indispensable in a successful love relationship.

He Learns from His Mistakes.

A man who admits his mistakes in such a way as to identify what he should have done better will learn and grow. He can also be counted on to help you with your problems. Too many men turn to stone when it's obvious that their woman is wrong and needs their help. The man who does this is usually not able to confront his own mistakes, let alone help others with theirs.

He Does Household Chores.

Research has shown that a man who does household chores as a matter of course, without bringing undue attention to himself, is much more flexible and loving in his relationship with a woman. This trait is especially important if that man is also a father. His example will help his children for the rest of their lives.

He Follows Through on His Responsibilities.

Although extroversion and adventurousness are the virtues most commonly appreciated at the outset of a relationship, it's conscientiousness that surfaces as the male's most important long-term trait in a successful relationship. Following through on responsibilities is contagious—it will help him be a success in work, play, and love.

He Admits and Faces His Fears.

Men often have a cultural block against recognizing fears. A good male love partner will willingly admit this block and will seek to overcome it by facing his fears, without using them to draw attention to himself. He will also demonstrate consistency in his efforts to overcome the feared object, person, or situation. A good example of this is the man who admits his fears of rejection when he thinks about reaching out to his father, yet consistently tries to improve his behavior in that regard.

23

He is a Kind and Considerate Lover.

Sex is both a mental and physical interaction. A good male love partner will learn what type of stimulation you enjoy and improve his skills in that area, again without drawing undue attention to himself. He will hold your hand in public places, hug and kiss you without immediately wanting sex, and engage in intercourse only after you've given him a signal that you, too, are ready.

He Controls His Temper.

Does your man make some attempt to profit from his anger? The "perfect man" finds a way to turn the energy of his anger into profitable problem-solving. He does that by stopping himself before his anger gets the best of him, by apologizing for his temper and indicating what he can do in the future to avoid it, or by walking away from a provocative situation and later examining what he could have done, if anything, to better handle the problem.

A "perfect" male love partner would score 20 points on this test. However, since I don't believe that a perfect score is possible, I suggest that you evaluate your man's score (and your own) using my 70-percent rule. It works as follows:

I believe that if seven out of ten interactions between love partners are productive—meaning kind, caring, and rational—they have a very acceptable relationship. If the percentage were to go up, they could move toward a truly special relationship. But if the percentage is above 50, the relationship will probably be good enough to keep either person from being terribly motivated to rock the boat. However, as the percentage moves below 50, distress begins to occur. Sadly, there are many couples who live in a 30- or 40-percent relationship over a long period of time, hoping it will change.

If he scored 15 or better, you don't need to confront him. If you want him to change a certain type of behavior or attitude, your best bet is to simply talk to him about it.

If he scored from 10 to 14, I doubt that you'll need to confront him. But if you do, concentrate on confrontations that are information-giving in nature. Such programs will be easy to identify once you get to Part II.

If he scored from 7 to 9, I doubt that he'll want to discuss his shortcomings, especially as they are judged by you. I suspect that your confrontations will have to be more action-oriented, and they will also take longer to become effective.

If he scored 6 or under, almost all the loving confrontations will give you a chance to explain your actions in a form your man might be able to hear. Capitalize on the moment when he says, "What's going on here?"

YOU:

You Are Self-Possessed.

It is unfortunate that femininity has always been equated with selflessness. In reality, a good female love partner should be able to talk about her life—her frustrations, dreams, and goals—without using the words "he" or "him" or otherwise making reference to a man.

You are Inner-Directed.

Many women are victims of learned helplessness, a culturally induced belief that they have no control over the things that happen to them. Women who are inner-directed will not give much credence to astrology or other indicators of luck or chance. They recognize that by controlling their actions and reactions, they can have an impact on the behavior of others.

You Understand Your Relationship with Your Father.

This is essentially the same as the trait listed for men. A good female love partner has an understanding of her relationship with her father; or, if not, she is able to talk about the sadness she feels without self-pity or hostility. She should not feel sorry for her father.

You Are Comfortable Being Self-Assertive.

Women have trouble with anger, just as men have trouble with fear. A good female love partner is able to confront her man

25

without becoming bitchy or guilt-ridden. She is able to remain problem-solving-oriented even when she is emotionally upset.

You Expect Sexual Gratification.

A good female love partner enjoys her body and the pleasures it can give her. She will be more likely to enjoy her sexuality if she views masturbation as an acceptable means of sexual gratification, although it may not be her preference.

You Follow Through On Your Responsibilities.

Conscientiousness is such an important virtue for a successful love relationship that it must be included in both lists.

You Accept Your Flaws without Guilt.

Too many women learn early in life to feel guilty about their mistakes. The guilt is not rational and it often doesn't lead to correcting the mistake, or even apologizing for it. Instead it causes a woman to suffer shame and low self-esteem. A good female love partner learns how to overcome, or at least control, this irrational guilt.

You Avoid a Judgmental Attitude.

During the last ten or fifteen years, women have been bombarded with information that encourages them to judge their men. Statements like, "He's just insecure," or, "He really doesn't realize how frightened he is of intimacy," are signs of arm-chair psychiatry, which has no place in a love relationship.

You Communicate Your Needs and Wishes.

A good female love partner is not afraid to ask for a hug, to ask her man to listen to her, or to give her support. She knows she deserves these things and is not defensive when asking for them.

You Do Not Tolerate Disrespect.

Our culture also teaches women to passively accept disrespect. This attitude can become so deeply ingrained that a woman will become anxious when a man does show respect for her. A good female love partner confronts disrespect or any sign of emotional abuse in a rational, direct manner.

If your score was 15 or better, I suggest that you use the self-preparation chapters merely to sharpen your skills. Pay special attention to any trait on which you scored a 0.

If your score was 10 or better, follow the loving-confrontation programs as they are laid out, but focus your efforts on the information-giving techniques I present in Part II.

If your score is from 7 to 9, take extra time in working through self-preparation. You may not want to make any major changes in the way you react to him (except to avoid emotional outbursts) in the next three weeks.

If your score is 6 or under, follow the directions for 7 to 9, but consider seeking professional counseling before confronting your man.

If your man wants to take this quiz, by all means encourage him to do so. However, be wary of arguments over discrepancies in scores, especially if he scored a 0 on "controls his temper." If you do discuss your scores, use behavioral examples to clarify your viewpoint.

The Knowledge Quiz

Self-management psychology—in which a patient becomes a student—is based on modern research. This research has yielded information that enables self-help to move from the speculative to the prescriptive. In order to become the best teacher you can be, you need to know why psychology can now give you exact answers to specific questions.

The questions below will help you assess your preparedness for change as well as acquaint you with some of the principles of today's psychology. Since this test isn't a laboratory research instrument, your score will not be nearly as important as what you will learn.

Read each question and select the option that comes closest to your opinion or to what you would do or say in the given situation.

1. If you got angry at your partner, which of the following would you do?
    a) Get it off my chest so that it wouldn't build up inside and get worse.
    b) Keep it inside until I could get a clear head and then get angry, trying to stay as rational as possible.
    c) Walk away without expressing my anger, calm down, and try to figure out why I got angry in the first place.
    d) Write down my angry feelings and then not mention the situation again.

2. When your partner does something that really hurts you, what's your belief about "forgiving and forgetting"?
    a) I never forget; it protects me from being hurt again.
    b) I eventually forgive, but I don't forget.
    c) I always practice forgiving and forgetting.
    d) I try to forgive, but I just can't quite do it.

3. Which of the following do you think best sums up the difference between men's and women's romantic attitudes?
    a) Women are more romantic, while men are more realistic.
    b) Women are both more romantic and more realistic than men.
    c) Men are both more romantic and more realistic than women.
    d) Men are more romantic, while women are more realistic.

4. If your partner were mildly depressed, which of the following actions would be *most* helpful to him?
    a) Go for a long walk together.
    b) See a funny movie or do something else to make him laugh.
    c) Leave him alone.
    d) Make him talk about the problem.

5. Which of the following statements best sums up your attitude?

    a) Often there is no way of protecting myself from bad luck.

    b) When I get what I want, it's usually because I've planned very carefully.

    c) I have often found that what is going to happen will happen.

    d) It's not always wise for me to plan too far ahead, because many things turn out to be a matter of good or bad fortune.

6. If you wanted to have greater trust in your partner, which of the following would you do first?

    a) Quiz him about where he goes and what he does during his free time.

    b) Remember back to a time I trusted him.

    c) Share some problems I had growing up and encourage him to do the same thing.

    d) Renew my trust by telling him that I trust him and asking if he trusts me.

7. If you and your partner broke up, which of the following would be the *most* important in making a reconciliation successful?

    a) Resolve all little spats before they become big ones.

    b) He doesn't go out with "the boys" and I don't go out with "the girls."

    c) Don't ever talk about why we broke up; let the past be the past.

    d) Say, "I love you," every day.

8. When your partner leaves for a few days on business or to tend to family matters, what's your reaction?

    a) I welcome the silence.

29

b) I'm thrilled. I can do whatever I want whenever I want without anyone nagging me or watching my every move.

c) I can't sleep at night or find anything that interests me. I'm lost.

d) I really miss him and count the minutes until he returns.

9. Which of the following statements do you consider to be "*wrong*"?

a) When things begin to go rough in my relationship, I can clearly see my part in it.

b) It seems to me that maintaining a smooth, functioning relationship is mostly a matter of skills, not luck.

c) If my relationship were a long, happy one, I'd say I was very lucky.

d) My partner and I can get along happily in spite of the most trying circumstances, if we decide to.

10. If you're feeling lousy about yourself, which of the following has the best chance of giving you instant relief?

a) Talk to someone about why I have low self-esteem.

b) Have my partner say he loves me.

c) Talk aloud to myself about what a good person I am.

d) Call my mother and have her tell me she loves me.

Answers

1. c) Walking away from anger and trying to figure out the cause is the best way to reduce the chances of anger resurfacing. The common notion that anger will build up inside until it explodes is harmful and misleading. Anger does not "build up" like interest on a savings account. If anything builds up, it's the intensity of angry *thoughts*, which, in truth, account for angry feelings. If you follow the basic law of learning—the idea that you *learn* to do what you do—then expressing anger will only teach you to be

more angry. The *anger management program* on page 53 will help you manage your anger so that you don't become bitter.

2. b) Too many women put pressure on themselves to forget about a past hurt. It can't be done, nor should it be attempted. A hurt will stick in your memory bank and fade with time. Hurts should be remembered, *if* the memories are used as lessons about life rather than reasons for self-pity. However, learning to forgive is good, not only because it promotes love and compassion, but also because it frees the forgiver from the yoke of holding a grudge.

3. d) A major study of romance and realism in young lovers found that men were more romantic—they brought gifts, strolled in the moonlight, and sang personalized love songs—whereas women, who were also romantic, were more realistic as well. While women enjoyed the gifts and the songs, they were more ready to grapple with the fact that love won't pay the bills.

4. a) Even in mild depression, there is a slowing of bodily functions. The majority of experts agree on the importance of a depressed person *doing something* to counteract this effect—doing meaning action. Some research indicates that bodily action removes acetylcholine—a chemical associated with depression—from muscle tissue. While trying to humor a depressed partner shows that you care, it doesn't have the positive physiological benefits of movement. Leaving him or her alone might be a good idea if he or she is only sad and expresses the desire to be left alone. I'm not a big fan of *making* anybody talk.

5. b) This is the only self-management statement of the four. The other three indicate a belief that luck or chance plays a major role in behavioral change. If you have trouble with this question, you should study Chapter 3, Being an "Internal" Woman, very carefully before proceeding.

6. c) Studies have shown that self-disclosure about family background, religious uncertainties, and past mistakes has a direct impact on increasing trust in a love relationship. As I've often said, a great relationship is built on the mutual sharing of weaknesses.

7. b) Saying, "I love you," every day couldn't hurt. Not talking about the reasons you broke up would definitely hurt. Too many couples triple their own stress by trying to solve every little spat that comes up; however, the best advice is not to make yourself angry in the first place over little things that are best left to fade away.

Research has concluded that one common reason reconciliations fail is because partners avoided solving their problems by going out with "the boys" or "the girls."

8. a) Because of changes in the world around us, you must face approximately one thousand times the amount of stress that your great grandfather did one hundred years ago. And if your relationship is distressed, you could probably double that number. If you're given the opportunity to spend a few days with the sounds of silence, cherish them. It is in silence that you can help your brain and mind cool down, reassess your self-management successes and failures, and get ready to reenter the struggle.

Although many people naturally miss their partner when he or she is away, waiting around will only diminish your chances of being more relaxed when your partner finally gets home. Getting angry will add to the stress.

9. c) This question is related to number 5. A long, successful relationship is the result of hard work, not luck or chance. Without a strong belief in this attitude, you can't be the best teacher you are capable of being.

10. c) Such simple statements as, "I'm a nice person," or, "My love is wonderful," can give a person an instant dose of self-esteem if said aloud. Of course, this verbalization must lead to constructive behavior change if the self-esteem is to become permanent.

SCORING. Add up your correct answers for an indication of your preparedness for loving confrontation.

7 to 10   You are very well prepared to help your man to change. Briefly review the next four chapters, and then begin to implement the programs. Chances are you've already given it your best shot, but one more try won't hurt.

4 to 6   This is a good score. Study Chapters 2 through 5, and work on any weaknesses you find in yourself. A few days of practice should adequately prepare you to implement a loving-confrontation program. Remember: go slow and be patient.

0 to 3   I suggest that you study the chapters in Part I very carefully before implementing the programs. It may take you a week or two before you'll be ready to begin. Likewise, each time you implement a program, your overall knowledge will increase, as will your ability to implement other programs.

No matter what your scores on the two quizzes are, your wisdom and knowledge have already grown and you're now ready to prepare yourself. You needn't worry about self-confrontation, because it can only make you stronger. If at any time you have second thoughts about the loving-confrontation programs, remind yourself that your purpose is to give your love the best possible chance of success. That will help give you the serenity you need to move forward.

Part I

PREPARING YOURSELF

2.

ACCEPTING YOURSELF

A major pitfall of practically all therapy (and most self-help books) is that the identification of mistakes can make you feel so depressed or angry that you wish you'd never discovered "the truth." Quite often the reason for this depression or anger is poor self-acceptance.

Barbara, a thirty-three-year-old loan officer and mother of two, seemed agitated after she completed the quizzes. She had done such a good job identifying the areas that needed change that I felt optimistic about her chances of helping her husband Doug. But she didn't share my feeling. The longer we talked, the more despondent she became.

Finally she spoke her true feelings. "I'm really the one who's responsible for my lousy marriage, aren't I? I mean, I didn't score very well on the quiz . . . I'm far from the perfect woman. No wonder Doug can't stand me."

When women like Barbara realize they've made mistakes, they often condemn themselves for being "wrong." They use the information we discover together to reject themselves. In essence, they say, "I don't have the right to have problems."

But you must give yourself the right to have problems. Accept-

ing your imperfections is *absolutely necessary* as a first step in changing undesirable behavior. In fact, none of the programs will be
effective for you and your relationship unless you apply the self-
acceptance program to yourself *now*. The method for doing this
is called *cognitive restructuring*.

Cognitive Restructuring

Cognitive restructuring is built on the principle that how we act
depends upon how we think. Cognitive therapists often refer to
the brain as a computer because the brain takes in information,
processes it according to programs, and then yields output in
the form of verbal and physical behavior. When that behavior is
troublesome, it is time to reexamine the programs, or attitudes,
that guide our thinking. If our attitudes are faulty, the computer
between our shoulders will faultily process information that will
lead to trouble in our output, or behavior.

In light of this theory, Barbara's lack of self-acceptance, and
attitude of not having "a right to be wrong" was irrational. All
humans *are* wrong from time to time. Barbara's belief in such
an irrational idea shows that she was operating with a faulty program and thus creating trouble for herself.

While the loving-confrontation programs are not based on any
one theory, my confrontation of Barbara's poor self-esteem was
an adaptation of cognitive therapy. I tried to help her rethink,
or restructure, one of her attitudes, or "cognitions." With a new
attitude, she would have a new way of thinking about imperfection. In time, she would learn to accept her fallibility and improve
the quality of her life. Once Barbara accepted her imperfections,
she would be free to correct them—and to demonstrate to Doug
how he could do the same. But for a real improvement in self-
acceptance, cognitive restructuring must be combined with another technique: *overt self-instruction*.

Overt self-instruction is the way in which the brain receives
new, more rational information with which it can better serve
an individual's needs.

"Basically," I told Barbara, "the lesson of overt self-instruction
is this: if you want your brain to retain a new thought or attitude,
make sure your ears *hear* and your eyes *see* that attitude.

"Here's what you do. Type or print on a piece of paper, 'I have the right to be wrong.' Tape it on your bathroom mirror. Every morning while you're getting ready for work, read the statement slowly aloud. Then turn away and say it again. Turn back and read it again. Repeat this process several times. The statement should be said aloud at least ten times each day. Depending upon who's around you, you may have to whisper it, but make sure your ears hear it."

I also explained another method of overt self-instruction, called *kinesthetics*. to Barbara. A good example of a self-accepting kinesthetic message would be an improved body posture that reduced tension. For example, while Barbara used overt self-instruction to talk aloud to herself, she was also to stand six inches from the bathroom wall and lean her back against it. She was then to push her abdominal muscles in so that the small of her back made contact with the wall, take a deep breath, and, as she let it out, feel the relaxation in her lower back. "Maintain that position and stand with your shoulders back and chin in," I told her. "Do both types of self-instruction at the same time and your self-acceptance will soar."

Barbara was skeptical. "It sounds kind of silly, talking aloud to yourself," Barbara said.

"Yes, it does," I agreed. "But brain research is telling us something that common sense supports. When we face a difficult learning task, our brain functions much better if it receives instructional input through auditory, sensory, and kinesthetic channels. If you think about it for a moment, you'll realize that overt self-instruction usually happens automatically. Picture a parent trying to put together a child's new toy on Christmas morning. He sits on the floor and reads the directions aloud saying, 'Put sprocket A into slit B, and tighten tab C with the enclosed wrench.' He is using overt self-instruction to maximize the problem-solving capabilities of his brain.

"Overt self-instruction is so simple it's difficult. However, if you use it to practice self-acceptance—saying positive statements about yourself ten times a day for at least two weeks—you'll begin to notice an improved attitude toward all your problems."

"Does it really work that easily?" Barbara asked.

"No, I'm afraid it doesn't," I replied. "We're only human, and we aren't as persistent and diligent as we'd like to think. Also, there are thousands of other thoughts flashing through our minds, competing for dominance. I've merely outlined the ideal. How it works for you depends on so many factors that it would take hours for me to explain them all. But believe me, *it does work!* And the more persistent you are, the faster it will work."

Automatic Thoughts

The biggest problem with using overt self-instruction to restructure your thoughts is being able to isolate an irrational thought from the millions of thoughts that flash through your brain without your awareness (for example, how to open a door, wash dishes, answer the phone). The following survey will help you identify automatic thoughts that may be hurting your self-acceptance.

Does any of these thoughts often occur to you?

Why can't I ever succeed?
I wish I were a better person.
My life's not going the way I want it to.
I'm so disappointed in myself.
I can't get things together.
What's the matter with me?
I'm a loser.
I'm a failure.
I don't have a right to be anxious (frightened, angry, etc.).

The more of these thoughts that flash through your mind, the more likely it is that you are experiencing poor self-acceptance.

Identify one of the thoughts listed above and reform it into a positive thought, the goal being to replace a negative automatic thought with a positive one.

For example, if, "Why can't I ever succeed?" seems to reflect your attitude best, rephrase it to say, "I can succeed at anything

I truly want." If, "What's the matter with me?" sounds a lot like what you say to yourself, rephrase it to say, "There's nothing wrong with me." Type or write that statement on a card, put it on your mirror, and use overt self-instruction to restructure your thought. Repeat the process with another negative automatic thought every two to three weeks.

The identification and alteration of automatic thoughts is the key to all areas of self-control. If your man won't change, you can be sure that he has many negative thoughts that are hidden from his consciousness. If you become proficient at cognitive restructuring—changing negative automatic thoughts into positive ones—you'll have a much better chance of teaching him to do likewise.

Toward the end of our first session, I noticed that Barbara seemed to be struggling with something. I interrupted my instructions and asked her what was bothering her.

"I'm having a tough time understanding how I must first accept my problem as okay before I can change it. When I say, 'I have a right to be wrong,' it sounds defensive, like I'm being selfish."

"If you were being selfish, you wouldn't accept the fact that you had a problem. In fact, that's what's wrong with Doug—he's being selfish by denying that he has a problem."

"But if I have a right to be wrong, then why should I change?" she said more pointedly.

"Because being 'wrong' is making you less effective in your own life as well as in confronting Doug."

"Then I *don't* have the right to be wrong, not if being wrong hurts the ones I love."

Barbara's logic called for a radical approach. "Quit playing God!" I told her emphatically.

"What do you mean by that?"

"You walk around thinking that you're supposed to be perfect in everything you do," I said. "There's no room for being human—making mistakes. I call that playing God."

Barbara sat in silence. Then a bright, relieved smile came to her lips. "Gosh, that thought feels good! To think I could learn to just let go and be a regular person!" She stopped speaking for a moment and then continued. "I see your point about how trying to be a perfectionist is playing God. And I've been doing it ever since I can remember. It doesn't make any sense, does it?"

"Absolutely not. There's one God; that's enough. Give yourself a break and join the human race."

Only when Barbara could give herself permission to have problems could she make a rational and conscious decision to do something about those problems. And only then would she gain the strength and insight necessary to confront Doug.

"The approach we are using can help you do a better job at being a loving human being," I said. "But first you have to give yourself permission to *be* a human being."

3.

BEING AN "INTERNAL" WOMAN

When Julie (whom you met in the introduction to this book) believed she had the power to "make" her husband Andy hurt, or to "give" him relief, she was behaving as if she had control over his feelings.

In self-management parlance, Julie had an *external locus of control*. In other words, she believed that people's feelings are caused by something outside themselves. If Julie were to realize that no one can control how a person feels except that person, she would be considered to have gained an internal locus of control. In other words, she would become an "internal" woman.

Research concludes that an internal locus of control corresponds to lower anxiety and a happier attitude toward life. Conversely, an external locus of control increases anxiety and results in a repetition of self-defeating behaviors. This is because an "external" cannot recognize the events leading up to bad feelings and thus avoid her own mistakes. *If you want to be successful in loving confrontation, you must become an "internal" woman.* When you do, you'll be able to say—and mean—"His problems are caused by *him*, not me."

Julie's poor self-acceptance and external locus of control put her in a no-win situation. When Andy was nice to her, she attributed it to luck or chance rather than to the fact that he had *chosen* to give her *what she deserved*. On the other hand, when he was insensitive, she would immediately ask, "What did *I* do to deserve this?" never confronting the fact that Andy caused his own sour mood.

Julie reacted as if a mysterious, evil force regularly reached out and thwarted her desire for happiness. Because she believed that feelings were caused by something beyond a person's control, she was helpless to do anything about her situation.

Julie, like so many women today, had been taught to be helpless. Fulfilling society's definition of femininity—as passive, submissive, and concerned with aesthetics—often necessitates learned helplessness, which entails a broad spectrum of attitudes in addition to an external locus of control.

I asked Julie to take two quizzes, explaining that they would help her evaluate her locus of control and learn how to overcome feelings of helplessness. You can take a quick reading of your general locus of control by honestly agreeing or disagreeing with each of the following statements.

To a great extent, my life is controlled by accidental happenings.

Often there is no chance of protecting myself from bad luck.

When I get what I want, it's usually because I'm lucky.

It's not always wise for me to plan too far ahead, because many things turn out to be a matter of good or bad fortune.

Whether or not I get to be a leader depends on whether I'm in the right place at the right time.

I have often found that what is going to happen will happen.

Whether or not I get into a car accident is mostly a matter of chance.

It's chiefly a matter of fate whether or not I have a few friends or many friends.

Each time you agreed indicated an *external* locus of control. If you agreed more than once, you should consider yourself leaning toward being an "external." The final answer, however, to whether you're an "external" or "internal" must come from within you.

Julie had to review her answers several times before admitting to herself that she was an "external."

"The first time I took the quiz," she said, "I was more interested in making a good impression on you than in being truthful with myself."

"That in itself," I said, "is an indication of being externally controlled. You think that if you please me, I'll like you, and my approval will be your source of good feelings about yourself."

I paused to let the logic sink in before continuing. "I don't control your self-esteem—you do. But if you do believe that I have such control over you, then you're helpless."

Julie was still confused when I asked her to take the second quiz. It applies the locus-of-control concept to love relationships. See if you agree, disagree, or are uncertain about each of the following statements.

When things begin to go rough in my relationship, I can see that I had a part to play in it.

It seems to me that maintaining a smooth-functioning marriage is mostly a matter of skills, not luck.

My mate and I can get along happily in spite of the most trying circumstances if we decide to.

I am often at a loss as to what to say or do when I'm in disagreement with my partner.

The unhappy times in our relationship just seem to happen regardless of what I do.

If my relationship were a long, happy one, I'd say I was very lucky.

An "internal" would have agreed with the first three statements and disagreed with the second three; an "external" would have answered in reverse.

"It's extremely difficult," I told Julie, "to sort out external from internal in relationships, because emotional involvement so often blurs objectivity. Even as an outside observer, I've found myself saying, 'Well, he said that she did after she said that he did . . .' in an effort to separate cause from effect. So no matter what you call yourself—external or internal—your ability to enjoy intimacy and happiness in a relationship depends upon becoming the best 'internal' you can be. It will reduce your learned helplessness and rid you of feelings of inferiority."

Internalizing Exercises

Here are three exercises you can do to increase your sense of internal control. Remember your goal: to realize that your feelings (as well as your man's) are caused by what you do and how you think.

1. I-am-something-without-a-man.

This controversial and eye-opening exercise is inspired by Dr. Penelope Russianoff's book, *Why Do I Feel I Am Nothing Without a Man.* Though simple, it can have a chilling impact. Here's what you do.

Find a private moment when you can speak aloud without being overheard or interrupted. Then, try to speak for ten minutes about your life *without making any reference to a man or using the pronoun* he *or* him. Talk about your past successes and failures, your current plans and projects, and your future hopes. Admittedly, you're forcing yourself to consider your life without what might be a very important part of it—your husband, boyfriend, male boss, or father.

Once you've struggled through those ten minutes (it will be easier if you're an "internal"), do it again; only this time, talk about your life *without making any reference to a woman*—daughter, sister, mother. As you search for words that are reflective of you as a person, you might begin to sense frustration. If you do, it's likely the result of being an "external," always looking *outside* yourself for the cause of what's happening *inside* you.

Doing the I-am-something-without-a-man exercise daily can sensitize you to the need to become internally controlled.

2. The Department Store Experiment

A more socially relevant lesson in internal control can be gained by conducting your own psychological experiment. It's a graphic demonstration of the principle that the way other people react to you depends upon your behavior.

You'll need an hour of free time, a shopping area with at least one large department store in it, a notebook, and a bit of acting ability.

The procedure is to approach a salesclerk in the department store and greet him or her in a predetermined manner; observe his or her reaction and write it down in your notebook. Do this three times with three different salesclerks, and use three different greetings. Here are my suggestions.

Happy. With a bounce in your step and a smile on your face, look the clerk in the eye and say in a peppy, energetic tone of voice, "Hello. How's it going? Maybe you can help me find what I'm looking for." You can then ask for a price or about the availability of an item.

Angry. With pursed lips and a furrowed brow, glare into the clerk's eyes and say in an angry voice, "I'd say hello, but I'm too mad to be friendly."

Depressed. With a downcast look and a defeated manner, make eye contact with the clerk and then look quickly away, saying, "I'd say hi, but that would probably go wrong too."

Now take your notes to a coffee shop and evaluate the outcome of your experiment. You should have found some differences in the clerks' responses to the different greetings. I suspect that the happy greeting brought a friendly response, the angry greeting caused the clerk to remain quiet so as not to incur your wrath (at least, that would have been a smart clerk's response), and the depressed greeting brought an empathic response. Take a moment to think about what caused the variance in their responses.

If you completed the cycle of three greetings at the same store and at approximately the same time, you reduced the influence of the environment upon the clerks' responses. Thus, the cause of the differences in their responses had to be what you said and how they took it. If there's any consistency in the responses to the three greetings (happy = congeniality, anger = silence, depressed = empathy), then you can tentatively conclude that the way you behaved was a major contribution to the clerks' responses.

While this isn't a foolproof experiment, it's adequate to teach you the lesson of internal control: your choice of behavior has a direct impact on how other people choose to respond to you. Obviously, there are two processes of choosing occurring in this brief encounter, yours and the clerk's. (A clerk who is depressed probably won't choose to be very empathic with your depression).

3. *The Puzzle Exercise*

There's one last exercise that will help you become an "internal" woman. It seems a little far-fetched, but it's based on solid research.

Make it a habit, when you have a few extra minutes, to pick up the daily newspaper and turn to the puzzle (crossword, anagram, or the like). You needn't solve it; just work on it for a while. Make whatever progress you can.

While you're working on the puzzle, turn your attention away from how you feel and focus all your energy on the task before you. During the first two or three weeks, use overt self-instruction to help you concentrate. "I can learn to solve part of this puzzle," "I'll get better every day," and, "What shall I do next?" are a few of the things you should be saying in order to turn your attention away from how the task makes you feel and toward what it will take to solve it.

Spend a few minutes at the start of this exercise checking the answers to yesterday's puzzle. Identify what you did right and learn from your mistakes; then say aloud, "Hey, I did pretty well, much better than last week. I'll do even better this week."

The goal of this exercise is to work on a project that requires mental effort but defies perfection. As such, it teaches you to

48

accept yourself as an imperfect person, which will generate feelings of honest pride. Many women categorically reject this suggestion because they are so bound by perfectionist thinking that they can't stand not being able to get all the answers to the puzzle. If you find yourself becoming obsessive about doing the puzzle, or unable to give it your best shot and walking away, simply do not attempt this exercise.

Internalizing exercises are more important for women than for men. According to research, female "externals" have more of a problem with learned helplessness than men do. If you're an externally controlled woman, you're probably going to have more problems in relationships than an externally controlled man.

It's my belief that women are genetically and culturally more able than men to make a deeper emotional commitment to a relationship, and that they are therefore more at risk if that relationship falters. If they are "externals," their helplessness will increase as love turns sour. Research seems to support this theory: after divorce, most women's external scores rise and remain high for approximately three years before returning to the predivorce level. Blaming others is their way of dealing with the grief.

Many best-selling books for women seem to support an external locus of control and thus prove damaging in the long run. Consider this quote from a recently published self-help book: "Once you learn the skills of this chapter, you'll have complete control over your mate's moods." I'm sure the author meant well, and wanted women to believe that they could improve their relationships. But what happens when a woman fails at controlling her man, which most assuredly will happen (remember that our experiment also had to take into account the influence of the clerk's personality)? The woman who thinks she controls her man's moods will damn herself for failing. Then, in an attempt to deal with her destructive guilt, she will frantically search for the answer to why her man is twisted and focus on how *he* caused the failure. More often than not, she will end up putting all the blame on him.

As you practice the restructuring of your thoughts to become an "internal," avoid the two extremes. If you think you have tremendous power to cause another person's moods, you will eventually be weakened by guilt and denial. On the other hand, if you think you have no control over what happens to you, you'll drown in a sea of bitterness. The end result of believing that you control either everything or nothing is that you have no control over the one thing that you *could* control—yourself.

Masculinity/Femininity

The Minnesota Multiphasic Personality Inventory (MMPI) is a popular and reliable personality test. One MMPI scale measures a person's masculinity/femininity (M/F). The M/F score can only be used to determine how well a person fits the traditional definition of masculine and feminine, not such things as whether a person is gay or lacks sex appeal.

Research has found that women who score high on the femininity scale also score high on learned helplessness. The implication is this: if a woman can reduce her femininity score, she can reduce her level of learned helplessness. Five items of the M/F scale have a direct bearing on internal control and skills of loving confrontation.

Keep two things in mind if you want to make these five items work for you. First, reducing your femininity score means *increasing your masculinity score.* Second, if you concentrate on only one or two of the five items listed below, you can take yourself out of the helpless category *without losing any of the feminine traits you and your man find attractive.*

Evaluate the degree to which each of these five behaviors, adapted directly from the M/F scale, are present in your life.

I frequently find myself worrying about something.

I feel that it is certainly best to keep my mouth shut when I'm in trouble.

My feelings are easily hurt.

I frequently wish I had the courage to stand up for what I think is right.

I prefer to solve problems in a covert and indirect manner.

The statement that most fits you is the one you should focus on first. If you're not sure where to begin, I suggest you begin with the last behavior, "I prefer to solve problems in a covert and indirect manner." Convert the statement into a positive goal. For example, "I should learn how to solve problems in a more direct and overt manner." Identify situations in which you can stop doing the "feminine" thing—making subtle hints, hoping your man will read between the lines—and start doing the "masculine" thing—telling him gently but directly exactly what you need and why. The indirect approach might be preferable in many situations, but dealing with a man who won't change is not one of those situations.

I cannot overstate the importance of developing an internal locus of control and reducing learned helplessness. Unless you begin to accomplish this goal (you don't have to *achieve* it, just *begin* it), you'll be unable to implement the loving-confrontation programs.

4.

CONTROLLING BITTERNESS

"I'm only thirty-eight," Betty said, "but I've already soured on men. I divorced Frank two years ago, after putting up with him ten years longer than I should have, and now I'm in a relationship with Tony. He can be a nice guy, but when he's with his friends he becomes a phony macho man, just like the rest of them. I could just slap him."

Betty was attractive; she had a keen sense of humor and loved dancing and good times. Although she had great potential as an excellent love partner, that potential was being destroyed by her bitterness.

Thousands of women become trapped in bitterness. The trap is sprung when they get angry at a man who won't change, even though their upbringing forces them to try to accept the situation. They see no way out of their anger, and the resulting frustration turns the anger into bitterness.

The *bitterness-control program* has four goals: to help you manage anger more effectively; to control self-pity; to reduce your frustration by helping you solve problems, instead of tolerating them or complaining about them; and to improve your confrontation skills by helping you learn assertiveness.

The Anger Management Program

Having anger is like having a body temperature of 101°. It's a clear signal that something is wrong. The standard advice today is to express your anger so that it doesn't build up inside. This is akin to telling a person with a fever to sit in a 160° sauna so that the outside of his body can experience what is happening on the inside. It doesn't make any sense. Worse yet, it's harmful.

One of the most fundamental laws of human nature is that we learn to do what we do. If we follow the traditional advice, we shouldn't be surprised to discover that we learn, in effect, how to be angry.

Anger is not a dirty word. If contained and rechanneled, it has an important place in loving confrontation. To help a man who won't change, you must learn to check your anger and then use it as a motivation to solve the problem that caused the anger in the first place. By containing anger in this manner, you can reduce angry outbursts to a tolerable minimum while maximizing your chances of getting his attention.

See where you currently stand in the management of anger by answering true or false to this five-point anger survey.

I am actually irritated more often than I let on.

I sometimes carry a chip on my shoulder.

I lose my temper easily but get over it quickly.

I seem to be a little rude to the people I don't like.

It makes my blood boil when somebody makes fun of me.

If you answered "true" to only one of these statements, your anger probably doesn't interfere with problem-solving. If two or three are true, you owe it to yourself and to the man you want to help to seek more effective methods of containing your anger. And if your score was four or five, there's a good possibility that your anger is out of control and that you should carefully study the recommendations I make in this chapter before moving on.

An in-depth research analysis of the aftermath of angry outbursts revealed that expressing anger almost always makes people feel worse. The interviewees reported such feelings as irritability, depression, aggravation, hostility, jitteriness, and unhappiness immediately after getting angry. When reviewing the results of the survey, one proponent of anger containment remarked, "This study should dispel the notion that expressing one's anger 'gets rid of' depression or irritability."

The *anger management program* begins with some information you will find useful in restructuring or clarifying attitudes.

- While women find it relatively easy to identify fears, they have a difficult time identifying their anger. Men seem to have the opposite problem. I expect that this is more than just a result of enculturation. Nature seems to provide men and women with complementary strengths and weaknesses, which is another way that it encourages us to stay together.
- It's inaccurate to view anger as a feeling that "builds up inside and needs to be released." Feelings are not stored as so much grain at wintertime; they are the results of thoughts. If you are happy, it's because you're thinking happy thoughts; sad feelings flow from sad thoughts; angry feelings are directly associated with angry thoughts. If anything is stored, it's angry thoughts. And if angry thoughts increase in frequency and intensity, angry feelings will follow close behind.
- Losing control of angry feelings is understandable. The goal is to get them back under control as soon as possible and then to look at why you became angry in the first place.
- Anger can become addictive. The more anger is expressed, the stronger the angry thoughts become. Hence, anger increases.

"Anger is healthy," I told Betty, "*provided* it leads to some attempt, however minor, to solve the cause of the anger. Therefore, if you get angry at Tony for his phony macho talk, your goal should not be to express your anger *or* to hide it, but to tell him that you are angry and to explain why. To accomplish this, you must do three things: contain your anger; do a little bit of self-analysis; and communicate without condemning.

"It's hard to accept," Betty said, "that anger is good."

"Anger is neither good nor bad, except perhaps in a moral sense," I said. "It's a neurological event signifying that your thoughts are arousing you. The tough part is figuring out what those thoughts are."

I went on to give Betty these steps to follow in managing anger:

- Reduce to a minimum the emotional outburst associated with anger. If you begin to yell, stop yourself as soon as possible. If you're too overwhelmed by your anger, remove yourself from the situation.
- Find a quiet room and pace. As you pace, count slowly aloud to one hundred.
- When you've finished counting, stop pacing and take two deep breaths, imagining yourself sitting on a deserted, sandy beach, soothed by the waves and warmed by the sun. (You will learn more about the calming effects of imagery in the next chapter.) Keep the image in your mind for two or three minutes, all the while breathing deeply.
- After three or four minutes, your anger should have dissipated. Return to your partner and continue your conversation. Tell him you're angry and specify the situation that precipitated your reaction. For example, you might say, "When you belittle women, I feel angry. I wish you'd avoid making references to women as sex objects when you get together with the guys."
- If your anger does not subside, then you are no doubt feeding it by ruminating on such thoughts as, "He had no right to do that to me," or, "How dare he treat me that way!" While you are still by yourself, speak these anger-provoking thoughts aloud and restructure them by saying, also aloud, "He's a human being; he has a right to make mistakes," or, "He treats me that way because he wants to feel a sense of belonging when he's with his male friends." Once you've contained your anger, return to your partner as in the last step.
- When you've successfully contained your anger and communicated your simple request, use the problem-solving pro-

gram that follows to thoroughly evaluate your conflict and reach a compromise.

"It sounds too easy," said Betty.

"It *is* easy," I agreed, "after you learn how to do it. But until you know how, it's like being a toddler taking your first steps. You fall down and try again."

Betty's path to managing her anger was a rocky one. Her first achievement was being able to walk away from an angry confrontation—an act I've come to label "calling time out." This, in itself, has cooled Betty's anger considerably.

Controlling Self-Pity

The biggest pitfall for anyone who wishes to manage anger more effectively is self-pity. If you respond to anger by pitying yourself—"Nobody has it as bad as I do"—you make it practically impossible to reach your man with any kind of rational communication.

If you've indulged in self-pity for a considerable period of time, you may be addicted to the warmth and comfort it can afford and not be aware of the damage it does to your self-esteem. Thinking, "It's not fair; oh, poor me," erodes your self-esteem by convincing you that you can't do anything about your problems except sit in a chair and complain.

If you'd like to confront your self-pity, try this innovative and daring strategy. Find an old, soft blanket in the back of your closet and buy a pacifier. Identify one remote corner of your house or apartment as the "pity corner." The next time you're sitting around feeling sorry for yourself, take the blanket and the pacifier off the shelf, go to sit in the pity corner, and suck on the pacifier and rub the blanket softly against your cheek.

I imagine that the very thought of doing such a thing makes you smile. *If so, you have already found the solution to self-pity.* Self-pity develops when you take yourself and life's trials and tribulations too seriously. The blanket-and-pacifier strategy graphically demonstrates the uselessness of self-pity and encourages you to find a solution to the problem instead of complaining about it.

You may resist, but I suggest that you try sitting in the corner at least once. Set the kitchen timer for ten minutes and come out when it rings. While you're sitting there, feel sorry for yourself *aloud*. Say all the self-pitying words—"It's not fair," "Oh, poor me," "Why me, God?" Realize that though self-pity may sound relatively harmless, it can be a destructive force in your life. Confine it to the small, obscure space of the pity corner.

You can use the image of the pity corner to counteract self-pity even when you're not at home. But if a mental picture of you sitting in the pity corner doesn't break the spell of self-pity, sit in the pity corner when you get home. If, for some reason, you enjoy the pity corner and don't want to come out after the bell rings, you have a problem that requires professional attention. Suspend the strategy and talk to a psychotherapist.

Systematic Problem-Solving

Once Betty had learned to manage her anger by calling time out, she needed to complete the other part of the bitterness-control program—reducing frustration by solving the problems that gave rise to the anger. I took extra time in instructing her in *systematic problem-solving*. This would give Betty the ability to think more logically and approach a confrontation with Tony on a more equal footing.

In addition to being an antidote for frustration, systematic problem-solving has the added strength of being perfectly logical. The analytical thinking of systematic problem-solving is very appealing to most men. Once Betty perfected the five simple steps, she had a better chance of enlisting Tony's participation in eliminating the source of her anger—his phony macho attitude. Even if he wouldn't cooperate, an increase in Betty's problem-solving skills would decrease her bitterness as it improved her self-esteem. It was a no-lose strategy.

"Involve Tony in your problem-solving program as soon as you can," I said to Betty. "Tell him you're going to solve the problem of what to do when he plays the macho role. Ask him for his help and participation."

I went on to outline the five steps involved in systematic problem-solving:

1. *Defining the problem.* Betty had to learn to define the problem in specific behavioral terms. For example, she might say, "When we're with a mixed group, you and the other men make snide comments about women as sex objects. You're always saying things like, 'There's nothing wrong with that woman that a good man couldn't fix,' or, 'I'd have to put a bag over her head.'" She should also tell Tony, "I need to do something instead of just sitting there and getting mad at you."

2. *Generating possible solutions.* Betty should write down on paper as many solutions to the problem as she can think of *without evaluating them*. This brainstorming should include any silly ideas or unrealistic possibilities. A sample list might look like this:

> Walk out of the room.
> Throw my drink in Tony's face.
> Scream, "You're all macho jerks!"
> Say, "Please don't talk that way in front of me."
> Do nothing.
> Sit on his lap and say something sexy in his ear.
> Go stand beside him, saying nothing.
> Punch him on the arm and kiddingly tell him to be quiet.
> Confront him after the party.

A complete list of possible solutions could number ten or more. A very important rule of systematic problem-solving is this: the quantity of solutions will increase the quality of the one you finally select.

3. *Projecting outcomes.* Betty should then project positive and negative outcomes for all the alternatives listed in step 2. For example, if she walks out of the room, Tony won't know what's wrong but she won't have to listen to his silliness. If she screams, Tony will dismiss her criticism and *she'll* look silly. If she confronts him after the party, he'll be more likely to understand her complaint, but she'll still have to listen to his silliness.

During this step, she will use her attitudes, biases, values, and physical and emotional resources to decide which of the alternatives are realistic *for her*.

Initially, Betty liked the idea of going over and sitting on Tony's lap, but then she realized that this act was likely to fuel further macho comments. As we talked, she began to feel good about a compromise combining three of the possibilities. She would go over to him and stand beside him in an attempt to interrupt his macho behavior; if that didn't work, she'd excuse herself to go to the bathroom and then confront him about his behavior after the party. (There is more about confronting macho behavior in Chapter 11).

4. *Implementing the plan*. Betty was to anticipate the next time she and Tony would be in a situation in which he would be likely to play his macho role. She wrote the words *macho plan* on the calendar next to a reminder about an upcoming party.

5. *Review*. Betty agreed to wait until the morning after the party to evaluate the outcome of her "macho plan." I reminded her that it might take several weeks, or until after the next party, before she knew whether or not her compromise solution had actually worked. If it didn't work, then she should go back to her list and try another solution or combination of solutions.

A woman who uses systematic problem-solving to cope with an anger-provoking situation and to reduce her bitterness is well advised to involve her man as early and as often as possible. If Tony could help Betty project and evaluate alternatives, he would probably become sensitized to the problem he was creating; this would make a confrontation unnecessary. On more than one occasion, this in itself has caused a man to change his behavior.

If you can get your man involved in helping you learn how to use systematic problem-solving to reduce your bitterness, you may actually solve two problems at once—your bitterness and his insensitivity to your problems.

Assertiveness

Assertiveness is defined as expressing thoughts that are consistent with your feelings. If you don't assert your thoughts and feelings to your partner, then you can't be much of a teacher.

Contrary to popular belief, assertiveness is not synonymous

with the expression of anger. In actual fact, the assertive person has learned to master anger by translating it into remedial action. Within the current scheme, assertiveness means simply to express thoughts and feelings to your man in such a way as to maximize the chances that he will listen to you.

Complete the following assertiveness checklist by rating how difficult it is for you to do each assertive behavior with each of the persons listed at the top. Use a scale of 0 = not at all difficult, 1 = somewhat difficult, 2 = very difficult.

Partner/Friends/Neighbors/Strangers

Requesting a favor from
Denying requests from
Disagreeing with
Giving compliments to
Receiving compliments from
Making complaints to
Receiving complaints from
Saying what you really think to
Saying, "I'm sorry," without guilt to
Maintaining eye contact with

There are two possible ways to score yourself: in terms of each person, or in terms of a total score. For our purposes, your assertiveness score with your mate is the most important.

Generally speaking, the more assertive you are with everyone in your life, the happier you'll be. It would be ideal if you scored 0 with your partner and under 5 with everyone else. However, if your partner score is under 5, your assertiveness is quite acceptable; if it's 6 to 10, you need to do some work; if it's 11 to 15, you should make assertiveness training a top priority; and if it's over 15, you may need professional help.

An overall score of 30 or less is good.

You should use the assertiveness checklist as a guide in improving your assertiveness. Your first step, however, is to accept the importance of being assertive. Get rid of the notion that you should be seen and not heard and replace it with an attitude that says that you must have the courage to let your man know where you stand on all issues important to your relationship. You may be thinking, "If I'm assertive, he'll see me as pushy and not love me." Restructure that thought this way: "If I'm assertive, I'll give him a real person to love and I'll avoid becoming boring or bitchy, both of which will result in him not loving me." This restructured thought will support you in times of doubt.

Now, turn your attention to the assertiveness checklist and those behaviors you judged to be most difficult for you. Say, for example, that you have a very difficult time disagreeing with people, especially your man. You can begin to improve your disagreeing by privately practicing the words you want to use.

You should be able to anticipate the situation in which you'll disagree with your partner. Select situations that are relatively free from emotional intensity (for example, the choice of a restaurant, rather than what to do about his pushy cousin).

If you've worked hard at your training, your disagreement may occur spontaneously. If you become tongue-tied halfway through the assertive statement, stop yourself, ask for a moment to collect your thoughts, and then proceed. If you've accepted your lack of assertiveness and given yourself patience and understanding, your assertiveness training will be successful.

Use the assertiveness checklist as a daily log of successful assertions. Place a check mark in the appropriate row and column each time you stated your thoughts or feelings in a rational, calm manner.

When disagreeing, keep these guidelines in mind:

- Focus on your reasons for disagreeing without justifying those reasons.
- Keep your words to a minimum.
- Avoid emotional outbursts.
- While you acknowledge the other person's viewpoint, don't abandon your own.

Here are some guidelines for other assertions:

- When asking for help, make your request specific and remind yourself that people like to help others.

- When receiving a compliment, simply say, "Thanks." If you deny an honest compliment, you've actually punished the person who's giving it to you.
- When complaining, be specific but don't attack; you leave the other person no way out.
- When making eye contact, look away from a person every 4 to 5 seconds.
- When saying no to a request, explain your reason once and keep it brief. If you don't want to share the truth, censor offensive bits of information rather than merely lying.
- When giving a compliment, say it once, keep it brief, and smile.
- When saying what you really think, you must decide whether or not you care enough about the person to share your honest feelings with him or her. There are many times when you won't care that much and therefore needn't say what you really think.
- A slight dash of humor is helpful in most assertive situations.

In summary, here's a brief review of the four essential elements of the bitterness-control program:

- *Anger Management.* Managing anger calls for a drastic reduction in the expression of anger and an increase in the control of angry thoughts. Turn the energy of anger into constructive problem-solving.
- *Controlling Self-Pity.* "Oh, poor me, I shouldn't have to tolerate this," can eat away at self-confidence as it stimulates depression. Confine your pity to ten minutes a day in the "pity corner."
- *Systematic Problem-Solving.* There are five steps entailed in mastering this all-important skill. Define your problem, generate alternatives and outcomes, set a timetable for implementation of a compromise, and review the actual outcome.
- *Assertiveness.* State your feelings and opinions without sarcasm or defensiveness. Learn to say "Thanks," to make eye contact, and to add a dash of humor. Practice with strangers before confronting an intimate.

Bitterness is a trap; it is unrelenting and sucks you deeper within itself each time your man treats you with disrespect and you do nothing about it. If you're working at accepting yourself, at becoming an "internal" woman, and at solving problems logically, you've already begun to escape the trap. Once you understand how to practice a confrontation, you'll be ready to stop, once and for all, the hurt and frustration that comes from loving a man who won't change.

5.

PRACTICING CONFRONTATION

Before Betty could have a successful relationship with Tony, she had to overcome a lot of bad habits from her first marriage. She had discouraged his suggestions that they get married, because she knew she wasn't ready to confront him in a constructive and loving manner.

Like all people, Betty profited from rehearsing her new behaviors before actually trying them out. This enabled her to desensitize herself to her fear of the unknown—to the worry of what Tony would say or do when she changed.

You, too, can profit from practicing a confrontation before actually using it. Practice won't make you perfect, but it will reduce the nervousness you'll face when doing something new. Follow these guidelines in order to make your rehearsal successful.

Be Relaxed

Relaxation is a stress-free state characterized by lowered heart and breathing rates, slower brain waves, and an overall reduction in the speed of metabolism. It's much more than taking a few minutes out of a hectic day and sitting down in a chair. Relaxation entails the systematic release of tension throughout your body with the ultimate purpose of gaining control over the things that are upsetting you.

The detailed procedure that, with practice, will make your relaxation successful is called *progressive relaxation*. It usually involves the systematic relaxation of twelve muscle groups from your face to your toes. However, there is a shortcut method that you might find successful. Here are the steps. (If you have a serious medical condition, ask your physician if this procedure is right for you.)

- Divide the muscles in your body into four groups: arms, face, neck through stomach, and legs.
- Find a comfortable and quiet place to sit, making sure the chair supports you completely.
- Take a deep breath, hold it for a few seconds, and then let it out slowly. Repeat this five or six times.
- First, focus on your arms. As you breathe in, tighten all the muscles in your arms and hands, making them as tense as possible. Hold your breath and the tension for 4 or 5 seconds, paying attention to how harsh the tension feels.
- Exhale slowly and let the muscles relax. Tell yourself to relax and let all the tension flow from your body. Focus on how wonderful relaxation feels.
- Repeat this process two or three times, each time noting the difference between the coldness of tension and the warmth of relaxation. Your arms will begin to feel heavy.
- Repeat the same cycle with the muscles in your face, torso and neck, and legs. When tensing one muscle group, try to keep the other groups as tension-free as possible.
- Once you've relaxed all four muscle groups, sit quietly and breath deeply. Each time your attention wanders, bring it gently back to relaxation by saying to yourself, "I give all the tension in my body permission to leave."

If you'd like to study relaxation in greater depth, buy an instructional tape recording at your bookstore. Some of the tapes have soothing background music or pleasant environmental sounds (ocean waves, nature sounds) that help to minimize distractions.

Until you learn deep relaxation, you should practice progressive relaxation once a day for a month. Eventually, you can achieve the same pleasant state of relaxation by playing a tape of environmental sounds through your earphones while sitting quietly in a comfortable chair and softly saying, "Relax," every minute or two.

Harness Your Imagination

Imagery is the ability to have a mental picture of something that's not actually present. It's a valuable skill that enables you to interact with many realities in your mind's eye before you meet them face to face. With imagery you can improve your courage, control your fears, build self-confidence, break bad habits, and change other aspects of your personality.

Because of a negative imagery history (for example, nightmares) or the absence of practice, some people may lack imagery skills. To determine your imagery ability, take the self-test below.

Ask yourself the following ten questions, giving each one a number according to this scale: 4 = very clear, 3 = moderately clear, 2 = fairly clear, 1 = unclear, 0 = no image.

Can you . . .

 . . . see a close friend standing in front of you?
 . . . see him laughing?
 . . . see his eyes?
 . . . see a blank TV screen?
 . . . imagine the sound of a barking dog?
 . . . imagine the sound of an exploding firecracker?
 . . . picture yourself lifting a heavy weight?
 . . . imagine the taste of lemon?
 . . . think of eating ice cream?
 . . . think of smelling a rose?

If your score totals 30 points or more, you should have no trouble using imagery techniques. If you scored from 15 to 29, you should pay special attention to the imagery exercise that follows. If you scored under 15, your imaginative powers are not currently at their best and the imagery exercise is a must in order for you to implement some of the programs to be recommended in Part II.

IMAGERY EXERCISE. Before beginning each exercise, sit down in a comfortable chair, take a few deep breaths, and relax.

First, place a favorite object (a golf club, a pair of shoes) in front of you. Look at it carefully. Close your eyes and picture it in your mind. Then open your eyes and look at the object again. Repeat this exercise for five minutes or until you can see the object perfectly in your mind.

Next, close your eyes and "see" your name spelled one letter at a time on a blank piece of paper. Imagine the first letter, look at it with your mind's eye, and then go on to the second and see it alongside the first. Do this until you can see your name in big letters on the paper. Practice five minutes a day.

Finally, with closed eyes, "see" a light bulb in a favorite lighting fixture. Imagine it growing brighter, then darker, and then brighter again. Then imagine that it becomes so bright that it illuminates the entire room. Five minutes of this exercise each day will further add to your imagery powers.

"Have you ever had a really great vacation?" I asked Betty as we concluded the imagery exercise.

"Yes," she said. "Early in my relationship with my ex-husband, we had a great vacation in Hawaii. He played golf and I just sat on the beach soaking up the sun and listening to the waves. I didn't even mind that he was gone all day. It was great."

"Can you close your eyes and picture that beach?"

"Absolutely," she said enthusiastically.

"I suggest that you buy a tape of ocean sounds, and whenever you get nervous about confronting Tony, sit in a chair, close your eyes, and relax. Play the tape and imagine yourself back on that beach. Do this for five or ten minutes, and *then* rehearse your confrontation."

Rehearse Your Lines

Behavioral rehearsal is a simple procedure that can mean the difference between success and failure in confronting your man. You can use it to practice assertiveness or any of the many programs you'll find in Part II of this book.

Betty used it to practice confronting Tony about his phony macho behavior. She found a room where she wouldn't be overheard or interrupted. After using her imagery exercise to relax, she thought of confronting Tony. Assuming she would spend the night with him after the party, she identified a target situation she would encounter the following morning.

She practiced saying several different things aloud, changing her words and her tone of voice as she went on. To make behavioral rehearsal successful, she had to use overt self-instruction (see page 38).

If you decide to rehearse your confrontation, you may wish to write a script of what you want to say and practice saying it to a picture of your man. Standing with good posture will add a kinesthetic element to your rehearsal. The more you rehearse your behavior (it should be a minimum of twice a day), the greater your chances will be of having a successful confrontation.

Though it's not absolutely necessary, you could add role-playing at this point to give your rehearsal an added lift. Find an understanding friend who'll act out the role of your man in the target situation. Say the words you used during behavioral rehearsal. Structure a situation that parallels the one you'll encounter and explain the kinds of things you want your friend to say. Each role-playing should last only long enough for you to say your words and respond to the person's reaction. After a few successful attempts, encourage your friend to try to catch you off guard. If you get tongue-tied or frustrated, simply stop the action and start over. Role-playing is universally applicable, because you can learn so much without ever really failing.

If your ultimate goal is to disagree with your partner, use reality testing to further prepare yourself. You can do this by testing your disagreeing ability with a person less threatening than your partner. A good place to start is with a salesclerk. It doesn't take much to disagree with a clerk about color, size, or suitability of an item. If you can't disagree in a rational way with a stranger, you'll find trying to do it with your man very frustrating. If your reality testing falters, go back to behavioral rehearsal or role-playing.

Reinforce Yourself

Loving confrontation requires that you have patience and tolerance with yourself as well as that you say and do nice things to yourself. Self-reinforcement is a way of being nice to yourself as it shapes you toward effective confrontation. Self-reinforcement is not the same as being selfish. The latter indicates an indifference toward others, whereas the former is a method of increasing your loving behaviors.

Self-reinforcement should follow the performance of a desired behavior. Some theories suggest that punishment should follow the failure to perform correctly or the performance of an undesired behavior. If the punishment is directly related to the reinforcement, a combination of the two is often effective.

There are endless ways of reinforcing yourself, both verbally and materially. Your way will depend upon what kinds of rewards you like. Two examples of material self-reinforcement are putting a dollar in a new-dress or new-golf-clubs fund for each chocolate cookie you replace with an apple (punishment would result in taking a dollar *out* when you eat the cookie); and ordering out for a pizza rather than cooking, after asserting yourself with your man. An example of verbal self-reinforcement is to say, "Good play," to yourself after making a good golf shot or winning a difficult hand in bridge.

You are now ready to begin Part II, "Confronting Him." Anxiety will be your biggest hurdle. The voice of anxiety sounds something like this: "What if I make a mistake and something goes wrong? I'm not sure I'll know how to handle it."

Let me tell you something that should help you deal with, and eventually rid yourself of, this anxiety: you need never again worry about making a mistake in confronting your man, or about being at a loss as to what to do or say, because there is no doubt about it—you *will* make mistakes and you *will* be at a loss as to what to do or say.

When you feel anxious, go into your bathroom, look into the mirror, and say, "I have the right to be wrong." Always keeping this in mind will increase your chances for a successful confrontation.

Part II

CONFRONTING HIM

6.

REALIGNING ATTITUDES

In Part II, Confronting Him, you will learn how to realign your attitudes in order to take the best approach to helping your man change; how to give your man information that may change *his* attitudes; how to react to him in a correct manner; and how to abandon a bad situation in order not to make it worse.

A confrontation does not have to be provocative in order to be successful. In fact, your most successful confrontations will be simple and low-key. Typically, they will involve giving your man information in such a way that he hears it and is encouraged to act upon it.

How to Use the Programs

- Always focus your attention on specific situations. Stay away from generalizations and give examples whenever possible. If necessary, keep a diary as a reminder of specifics.
- Whenever possible, apply a program to a situation that's moderately, rather than highly, distressful. For example, do not confront his insensitivity by attacking him in the sensitive

area of his unwillingness to please you in bed; you'll only inflame a tense situation. Instead, use the *househusband-shaping program* to confront the less distressful issue of his insensitivity to your need for help around the house.

- Never confront in the midst of an argument. Let things cool off before you implement a program.
- Consistency is most important in loving confrontation. Most of the programs will have an immediate impact, but it will take anywhere from two weeks to six months before you'll see the whole effect. Therefore, once you find a program that feels good to you and seems to be having an effect on your man, stick with it. Don't be surprised if you find yourself modifying it to suit your individual needs and personality.

Risks of the Programs

Any prescriptive program contains risks. Here are a few to keep in mind:

- You may learn that your man doesn't love you enough to work toward change. If that's the case, you'll be facing sadness (but not guilt) over this loss of hope.
- Because the teacher usually learns just as much as, if not more than, the student, the programs will undoubtedly teach you some things about yourself that you never knew. Any risk of this hurting you will be minimized if you regularly practice the self-acceptance program.
- Treating yourself with more respect may result in your man respecting you more. I know it sounds preposterous, but if you've gotten used to disrespect, being treated with respect may give you an uneasy feeling. However, if you stick with it, you'll get used to the new feeling very quickly.
- If your loving confrontation is successful, your man may criticize you in ways he never has before. Whereas he once thought he had to protect you from his opinions, he may now feel confident in saying what's on his mind. This may prove disturbing at first; but then, isn't this kind of honesty what you *really* want?

- A confrontation program that fails may bring you face to face with your fears of being rejected, financially distressed, and alone. However, you will also have the courage and determination to overcome these fears.
- Since each of the programs is catalytic—you stimulate a reaction without being able to control it—your man's reaction may not be exactly what you predicted. But if you've prepared yourself well in Part I, you'll be able to say, "I can handle whatever happens. At least it won't be boring!"
- The programs rely heavily upon *demonstrating* the behaviors or attitudes you desire. *Modeling*, as psychologists call this demonstration, exposes you to ridicule. If you go slowly, you'll identify the ridicule early and be able to avoid it.
- You may find yourself using diary notes to try and win an argument or "prove" that your man is wrong. If so, suspend note-taking immediately and apologize to your man as soon as you can.

You'll be able to handle the side effects of any program, provided you've mastered the tasks laid out in Part I, "Preparing Yourself." In designing the programs in Part II, I've kept the "stability factor" foremost in my mind. That is, in implementing the programs, you won't run any substantial risk of making a bad situation worse. The worst that will happen with any loving-confrontation program is that it simply won't work.

If you become the best teacher you can be and follow the guidelines listed above and throughout this book, your relationship will change. *There's no doubt about it!* This change will produce one of three possible outcomes:

1. Your help will stimulate growth in your man, and your relationship will improve (though marriage counseling may be needed). Or . . .

2. Your help will be met with indifference or hostility. However, if you persist in confronting both yourself and your man, you'll realize that these factors are far outweighed by your desire to seek a happier life. Or . . .

3. Your loving confrontation will help you realize that some

of the disrespect you thought was coming from your man was actually *coming from yourself.* Once you give yourself more respect, you'll find you are less hurt by some of your man's behavior and more realistic in your demands. He, in turn, will be more likely to comply with these requests.

No matter which of the above outcomes awaits you, your love life will never go around in circles again. That's why loving confrontation is a no-lose program.

7.

IMPROVING COMMUNICATION

Although it's often overused, the recommendation, "You need to improve your communication," is still the most important one for a distressed relationship. Most men recognize the need for improved communication, while considering it to be their woman's responsibility. They believe that if they are a good provider, the relationship will take care of itself. It does little good to lecture these men about the conjoint nature of improved communication. They have to be shown. Steve was a case in point.

We Don't Talk Anymore

Steve and Kristy had been married for eight years. As an international businessman, Steve could send information halfway around the world in a matter of seconds, but he had a terrible time communicating with the person who slept twenty inches away from him. Without the connection that arises from effective communication, their once-intimate relationship was fast becoming a partnership of strangers.

"I don't know where to begin trying to reach him," Kristy, who was thirty-three, told me. "I'm a public relations consultant, and communication is my business. So why do I feel like I'm back in the first grade."

Steve accompanied Kristy to our first session, but he was guarded and cynical. His view of marriage counseling was similar to that of many men. He saw it as a waste of time and money, but was willing to participate as long as it made his wife happy. However, he found excuses for failing to attend subsequent meetings. I had no other alternative but to help Kristy improve the communication in her relationship without the active cooperation of her man.

"You may not need marriage counseling to improve your communication," I told her. "You might be able to use some simple techniques to help Steve learn to apply his global communication skills to his marriage."

Kristy was skeptical. "I told you before, I've tried everything. And now I'm at the end of my rope."

"You've got to quit trying so hard," I countered, gently but firmly. "I watched you in the first session. You were driving yourself nuts. You acted as if the future of the world was on *your* shoulders. I saw how Steve sat back and let you do all the work. You were busting your butt to improve communication, and he was playing devil's advocate, saying, in effect, 'No, that won't work; no, that won't either.' By trying to do it all, you're just proving what he already thinks—that keeping the marriage together is your job.

"The only realistic thing you can do is to implement the latest research-proven techniques; and if they don't work, then accept the fact that your man has a problem you can't do anything about."

Kristy looked at me as if I'd just stolen her favorite doll. Her response surprised me. "You know, my best friend has been trying to tell me that for months. I guess I'm just confused about how to approach Steve."

Positive Communication Checklist

I suggested to Kristy that she use a softer, more upbeat approach to improve communication within her marriage. Perhaps she could use a quiz to pique Steve's interest in working at their relationship. The program that worked for Kristy might work for you.

The *positive communication checklist* is made up of twelve verbal and nonverbal behaviors that, when implemented, characterize a complete communication system. I've converted the checklist into a quiz that you can use to improve communication in your relationship.

When you take the quiz, rate your own behavior as you remember it from a recent conversation. Answer each question using a three-point frequency scale: 0 = never, 1 = sometimes, 2 = frequently.

Did you (nonverbally) . . .

. . . nod your head positively?

. . . lean forward toward your man?

. . . maintain regular eye contact?

. . . refrain from scratching your face or touching your hair?

. . . refrain from crossing your arms and legs?

. . . sit still in the chair?

Did you (verbally) . . .

. . . stick with an issue?

. . . avoid interrupting?

. . . use a soft, caring tone of voice?

. . . help keep talking time equal?

. . . avoid put-downs or personal attacks?

. . . share personal viewpoints?

Rather than focusing on your score, vow to improve it by increasing each positive type of behavior. I've purposely excluded categories for interpreting the scores because I don't want your man becoming defensive about this very important checklist. The objective of the quiz is *not* to sit in judgment of him, but to entice him into a fun-filled exercise that will sensitize him to the twelve behaviors necessary for effective communication.

Take a gamelike approach to the checklist and avoid making it seem like a life-and-death exercise. Show your man what you're doing and be willing to get his feedback on your self-evaluation. Then say, "Why don't you give it a try?"

If your man rates himself higher than you think is warranted, don't judge him. Instead, assume that he's trying to tell you something. He may be trying to say that he's not as bad as you think he is, which actually is another way of saying that he cares about improving communication.

If you disagree with his rating on a particular item, ask him what he remembers doing or saying. Then tell him what *you* remember, but do not tell him that his memory is incorrect. If you find yourself wanting to prove you are right, remember: the reason you're going through this exercise is to *improve* future communication, not to decide who has the best memory.

Throughout this exercise, remind yourself that you're not in control of your man's attitude. You're a teacher, and your best tool is to use yourself as a model of excellence. Don't take responsibility for your student, but don't sit in judgment of him either, especially if he refuses to learn. If you treat your man as if he's a fragile vase, then you're acting like an "external" woman, believing that you are somehow responsible if he gets offended.

Basic Communication Script

I'm not a big fan of giving anyone the exact words to use during a confrontation. However, you might face a situation in which you need a few words to get you started in the right direction. If so, remember the *basic communication script*. It's a generic outline of the words to use that will promote the greatest possible communication of ideas while minimizing misunderstanding.

Here is the basic script:

"When you say ————, I think (feel) ————. I wish you would ————." When responding to your partner's opinion, say, "When you say that, I think (feel) ————. I do (don't) agree with you, because ————."

This is an elementary script, and you should feel free to expand upon it. If you change certain words (for example, *opinion* to *request*), this script can help you make compromises and resolve conflicts. Converting feelings into a request and proposing compromises can result in an active discussion of more complex issues, thus building a foundation for mutual satisfaction.

Type the script on a piece of paper and let your man see it. Explain exactly what you're doing by making reference to my recommendation. This will help offset the fact that the script gives your conversation a stilted tone. Encourage him to use the script when responding to you.

The basic communication script is limited, but when you're attempting to overcome poor communication habits, you need an elementary method that insures that both of you are operating within the same system. Once you understand the basics, it'll feel natural to say, "I feel bad because we're not talking as we used to. Can't we work at that?"

Five Ways to Improve Communication

"Last night," said forty-year-old Jackie, trying to hide her bitterness, "I asked Pete to talk about our income taxes. He said okay—as soon as he took a package over to the neighbors. But he was gone for over an hour, and by the time he got home, I was so busy I forgot to say anything. It's getting so we never talk anymore.

"I know it's not all his fault," she went on with a sad smile. "I should make more of an effort. But when I do, it doesn't do me much good. So I go ahead and do what has to be done. Then, when a problem develops, Pete says, 'Why didn't you talk to me about it?' And I get so frustrated that I just throw up my hands and walk away. If I tell him I tried to talk to him about it, he just denies it."

Jackie's and Pete's problem is not unlike that of many modern couples. They are so busy with day-to-day survival that they forget the fundamentals of communication. If they don't start making time for intimate contact, the psychological distance between them will continue to grow.

I gave Jackie five techniques that she and Pete could use to confront the breakdown of communication in their relationship. You can use one or a combination of any of the following to confront one of the most typical problems in any relationship—"We don't talk anymore."

APPOINTMENT. If you and your man are barely able to wave as you scurry past each other, I suggest you make an appointment to talk to each other.

The appointment should be given the same degree of significance as a regular work appointment. Agree on a time, place, and topics (for example, taxes, child-rearing, and buying a new dishwasher). Be prepared to move the conversation away from specific problems and into a discussion of your estrangement. But always keep the conversation as objective as possible. For example, discuss ways to schedule regular periods of conversation instead of trying to figure out who's responsible for the lack of communication.

Avoid places where you'll meet friends. (If you have a luncheon meeting, make sure you get a quiet table.) And permit no interruptions. If it's uncomfortable at first, use notes to guide your discussion. Use problem-solving (see page 57) to keep your conversation rational and positive in tone.

If you and your man are successful in "reconnecting" through stimulating conversation, an interesting problem might develop. You'll be likely to experience the warmth of intimacy, which in turn can lead to sexual desires. Therefore, don't schedule any meetings after lunch that can't be canceled.

BIBLIOTHERAPY. This procedure is designed for couples who are in mild distress. For each partner, it entails reading a section of a mutually enjoyable book and then discussing the contents and individual reactions. You can each read the same biography and then compare reactions, or each of you can read a relationship-enrichment book and talk about what parts of it might apply to your relationship.

READING ALOUD. This technique is similar to bibliotherapy except that you read aloud to each other. In most cases you will have to begin the reading aloud with the hope that your man will eventually follow suit. If he doesn't, that's okay. You can still accomplish one goal: your man will hear you speak with a kind, upbeat voice, a voice that is free from problems or complaints.

You can start by reading him an interesting section from a magazine or newspaper. If that's successful, you might read him a few pages from a book each night before going to sleep. An example of the ultimate goal of reading aloud would be for the two of you to act out a play together.

ACTIVE LISTENING. This technique helps you demonstrate to your man what you would like him to do when you're talking.

The next time he begins to speak, drop what you're doing and listen to him. Do not speak any of your own thoughts or interpret what you hear. Ask for repetition by saying, "Please say that another way," or, "Say it again, I think I missed something." Obviously, active listening won't last long if he says, "Please pass the sugar." It works best if he's explaining a problem he had at work or stating his opinion about a recent event.

After ten or fifteen minutes, feed back what you've heard by summarizing his points. Then ask him if your summary is accurate.

To encourage him to listen to you, don't be afraid to say, "I just want you to listen to me for a few moments. Could you please put the newspaper down?" Your active listening will increase the chances that he will ask you about yourself, and you'll get to express your ideas or opinions without fear of contradiction or, worst of all, being ignored.

Many couples have found that active listening can spark spontaneity and increase the satisfaction of a conversation. The more you can control extraneous interruptions, the greater the success of active listening.

If active listening is successful, you'll begin to feel a deep sense of tranquility during the middle and latter stages of the process. This peace comes from two sources: your brain, which enjoys having the auditory channels stimulated without the static created by arguing or needing to think and respond with new information; and your mind, which relaxes when you immerse yourself in another's agenda. Active listening gives your ego defenses a welcome rest.

PASSIVE QUESTIONING. Begin this technique by saying, "I'd like to ask you some questions, is that okay?" Even his yes is a connection, however small. Ask him about the particulars of whatever he's talking about. For example, "What kind of things would make you feel better," or, "At what point did you realize things were not going well?"

If you can't be sincere in this questioning, don't do it. Avoid sarcasm or questions that mask a confrontation ("Don't you think that you were wrong?"). Also, avoid any question that stimulates disagreement or argument, and do not push the conversation in a particular direction.

Passive questioning is to be used only after both partners have contained any anger that might be present. You need a clear head in order to weigh evidence, sort through alternatives, and project probabilities.

Other approaches to passive questioning include looking at the bright side ("I know it sounds strange, but is there a good side to your problem?"); looking at the reason for defenses ("Are you hurt about something?"); and trying to help ("What can I do for you?" or, "Is there anything I can do to help?").

In summary, here are five simple techniques you can use to try and improve the communication between you and your man. You need only minimal participation from him to get each one started.

- Appointment. Make a luncheon date and discuss minor household problems. It could lead to another, more serious conversation.
- Bibliotherapy. A mild form of structured communication designed to stimulate problem-solving (hence the idea of *therapy*).
- Reading aloud. He hears your voice with pleasant tones reading him something he finds interesting.
- Active listening. You demonstrate the kind of full attention

to his part of the conversation that you'll eventually ask him to show you.

- Passive questioning. You demonstrate a more active form of conversation, giving him a chance to expand upon his thoughts. Later, you'll ask him to reciprocate.

When It's Hard for You to Talk About Sex

Nothing is more difficult for two people to talk about than their sexual frustrations. It's unfortunate, but the subject can introduce immediate estrangement into an otherwise secure relationship. A major reason for this is that you and/or your man could be afflicted with a debilitating phobia.

I'm sure you already know that public speaking is the number-one fear in our society. Recent studies suggest that the same kind of fear might be present during communication within a relationship. Therefore, your fear of talking to your man may exist *regardless of the subject*. If you add to that the fear of rejection associated with talking about a sensitive subject (you can't get more sensitive than your sexual frustrations), you could be dealing with a phobia. And if you have trouble in this area, there's an excellent chance that your man's fear is even greater than yours.

Below is a brief survey that will indicate your degree of apprehension in speaking to your partner. Rate each statement on a 5-point scale: 1 = strongly disagree, 2 = disagree, 3 = not sure, 4 = agree, 5 = strongly agree.

My thoughts become confused and jumbled when I'm discussing issues important to my partner.

I usually try to work out problems myself instead of talking them over with my partner.

Even in casual conversations with my partner, I feel I must guard what I say.

I am hesitant to get into casual conversation with my partner.

I am uncomfortable getting into an intimate conversation with my partner.

If your total score is under 9, your apprehension in speaking to your partner is low. If it's over 17, your apprehension is high. Whatever your score, if *you* think your apprehension is too high, you'll want to review the relaxation and imagery programs outlined in Chapter 5.

Hillary's score was 21, confirming what she already knew— that her fear of speaking to her husband Jim was very high. "Most of my fear of talking to Jim centers on sex," she said. "He seems to be very content, but I'm not. I've had two orgasms in all the time we've been having sex. I want to talk to him about my frustrations and my needs, but I don't know how."

"You don't know how?" I asked. "Or are you afraid to say the words?"

"Well, it could be both, but it's mostly being afraid. My fear makes it difficult to remember the words."

Hillary was a quietly attractive attorney in her mid-thirties, but she looked and sounded as if she were a high-school sophomore going on her first date. She explained that she and Jim were compatible in many respects. They were both attorneys, didn't want children, enjoyed skiing, and preferred sitting home in the evening and reading to going out. But when it came to talking about their personal lives, Hillary felt anxious. The more personal the subject matter, the closer to the breaking point her anxiety would become.

Desensitization

I instructed Hillary in the general theory of *desensitization*, a self-management procedure that teaches a person to become less sensitive, or desensitized, to a frightening situation. Here is an outline of a desensitization program that can be adapted to fit a situation similar to Hillary's.

The program begins with the realization that you're not alone. The thought that many other bright women share your apprehension will help you be less embarrassed by your fear. The other thought that might help is this: chances are very good that your man also has a fear of talking with you about such intimate topics as sexuality. However, his fear is buried much deeper than yours.

Use behavioral rehearsal (see page 68) to practice saying the words you want to say. Be sure to rehearse aloud. Of course, saying the words to your partner will be much more difficult, but getting used to the words themselves will make the actual conversation easier.

The most profitable part of the program is the utilization of imagery (see page 66). After assuring yourself that you have good imagery skills, find a quiet ten minutes to close your eyes, relax, and imagine the following: you and your man are sharing an intimate, loving moment, sipping a glass of champagne. You exchange words of past romance, present love, and future hope. It seems natural for you to say, "Let's go make love and see how long we can make it last."

Experiment with a variety of statements, using the pronoun *we* and expressing your needs within the context of erotic love-making plans. As you imagine this scene, see yourself as deserving sexual fulfillment and tell yourself that if your man loves you, he'll be excited to learn how to satisfy you.

There are three things that can go wrong with this imagery. First, if you're afraid of your sexuality because of an early-life trauma (for example, you never resolved being sexually abused), the imagery will result in an increase rather than a decrease in fear. Also, if your man doesn't love you, your sharing may force that fact to the foreground and result in a whole new set of problems. Likewise, if your partner has a sexual problem, your open discussion may cause him to "deal" with his problem by blaming you.

The general rule to follow is this: don't use imagery to desensitize your fear of sexual sharing (or any fear, for that matter) if the process itself makes you feel worse. In other words, if there's pain, there's no gain.

If the imagery is successful, your fear of talking about your sexual needs will begin to subside within a few weeks. The more you experiment with imaginary situations and ways of stating your needs, the easier it will be to actually approach a situation with your man.

As you continue to practice the words and imagine the scene, look for an opportunity to create a scene that parallels the one you've been imagining. Remember: you're not intending to dump the issue on your man in ten seconds or less. You want to create a loving, mutually accepting situation during which the conversation can naturally turn to sex. It will be easier for you to mention your sexual needs as an adjunct to a "sexy" conversation than to make them the main attraction. Honesty in sharing doesn't preclude the use of tact. You needn't force yourself to be honest by saying, "I want to tell you how sexually frustrated I am." This so-called honesty actually sounds like a diagnosis or a condemnation of his love-making ability.

It's perfectly understandable if you want to delay the implementation of this recommendation. Don't rush a fear; you risk making it worse. Anyhow, the use of behavioral rehearsal and imagery may result in a greater acceptance of your sexual self, which in turn may allow you to open yourself to sexual pleasure, which is exactly what you want. If the first part of the program is successful, you might not have to complete the second part.

He Doesn't Know How to Talk to Me

"He treats me as if I'm stupid," thirty-year-old Jane complained. "He says he shouldn't even expect me to understand what he's saying. I'll find him talking to other women about his work, but not to me. Just because I didn't graduate from college, he thinks I won't understand. But I'm just as smart as the women he talks to."

Jane was a slender woman whose long blond hair and innocent blue eyes gave her the "cheerleader look." Her husband Joe was a thirty-one-year-old, highly successful computer-software salesman. Jane had worked to put Joe through his last year of college, and within a few years he had become the *wunderkind* of his firm. Jane enjoyed her work as a secretary in the local hospital, and she and Joe were planning to start a family.

"You sound quite defensive," I said, reflecting on her weak tone of voice when she compared herself to other women. "I can see why you'd feel intimidated, but you need to remind *yourself,* not Joe, of your intelligence."

"But he makes fun of me," Jane said. "What am I supposed to do, ignore him?"

"I know it may not make much sense," I said, "but one of the first things you should do is realize that his making fun of you probably represents his lack of skills, not yours."

"Joe?" she said in disbelief. "The youngest regional manager in the history of his company? *He* lacks skills? What have you been drinking, Dr. Dan?"

"I don't mean work skills," I clarified, "but skills in disclosing his thoughts to someone with whom he feels vulnerable. In short, he may not know how to talk to you."

It's not uncommon for a man, especially one who's been successful in the business world, to have a simple skill deficit—he doesn't know how to talk to someone he loves. To cover his deficit, he may belittle his woman, criticizing her for the very thing he lacks—understanding.

"The truth of the matter might be," I continued, "that Joe is the one who feels stupid, at least when it comes to communicating with his wife."

If Jane's dilemma reminds you of yours, the first thing you should do is to avoid becoming defensive. You can use overt self-instruction (see page 38) to remind yourself, "I'm not stupid when it comes to communicating with my man." If you post this on your mirror and repeat it ten times a day, it will not only have a positive effect on your view of yourself, but it will also stimulate your man's inquisitive nature. When he asks you what you're doing, you'll have a perfect opportunity to explain your actions *and* your complaint.

Second, improve your assertion skills as they apply to communicating with your partner (see page 59). This will make it very difficult for him to criticize you unjustly, and it will motivate him to overcome his deficit. (Posting the self-statement and explaining it to him become very important to the achievement of this goal).

Third, learn or improve upon the following six *communication skills*. Your improved skills will serve to confront your man's lack of skills as well as teach him how to talk to someone he loves.

IMPROVE YOUR POSITION STATEMENTS. Say, "This is how I see it," to add clarity to the things you want to say. Also, reduce the total number of words you use when explaining yourself.

ASK FEWER QUESTIONS. Surprisingly, it has been found that assertive lovers refrain from asking questions—except when using passive questioning. If you reduce your questions, you avoid asking questions that are actually disapproval in disguise. For example, "What can't you understand?" "How many times do I have to tell you?" "Why do you keep giving me that strange look?" These are inflammatory; they move the discussion toward hurt feelings and argumentation.

DECREASE VERBAL DISAPPROVAL. "You never try to see it," or, "You're always too quick to jump to a conclusion," are examples of unnecessary disapproval. Whenever possible, follow the old adage, "If you can't say something nice, don't say anything at all."

INCREASE VERBAL APPROVAL. "Thanks for understanding," and, "I appreciate your listening," are examples of verbal approval.

INTRODUCE COMPROMISES. "Well, I see your point, but I still think my point has to be dealt with." "I hear what you say"—(rephrase his comment)—"and I can agree with part of it"—(spell out that part)—"but is there room for my point?"

TOLERATE NEGATIVE EMOTIONS. The goal of any couple who wish to maximize their communication is to be able to express negative emotions without the other partner taking offense. If your man gets upset with your confrontation, say, "I'm sorry about your hurt," not, "I'm sorry I hurt you." The first statement reflects an internal locus of control. You express empathy without attributing causation. The second is an "external" statement, which often leads to guilt.

"Why do I have to do all the work," Jane asked, "when you say that he's the one with the deficit?"

"You're not going to do *all* the work, or at least I hope not. You'll do your part, with the hope that Joe will learn to do his. Anyhow, you love him and you're trying to help him."

Feeling she was about to give her man her best shot, Jane smiled, sat back in her chair, and said, "That's the best reason of all, isn't it?"

8.

COPING WITH HIS TEMPER

If your man believes that feelings are just more hard data to be collated, filed, and transferred from one terminal to another, he may also believe that arguments somehow result in constructive communication. In truth, however, the only good argument is one that's stopped before it has a chance to create bad feelings. If your man has this blind spot, it'll be up to you to teach him the benefits of avoiding arguments. But, as Mindy found, that's not as easy as it sounds.

If He's Always Arguing

Mindy, a bright, sassy thirty-five-year-old woman who was a full-time wife and mother, was leery of confronting her man, no matter how indirectly.

"Mel can be a sensitive and loving man," Mindy explained during the first of two orientation sessions I had with her. "But he has a quick temper. It seems as if he doesn't want me to confront him about anything. If I say something to him at the wrong time or in the wrong way, he starts an argument.

"Last night," she continued, obviously upset, "I told him that he'd forgotten to get salt for the water softener. He looked up from his magazine and said, 'Can't you handle anything?' When I asked him what he meant, he said that I'd had plenty of opportunity to get the salt. So I reminded him that he'd told me he was going to get it. He denied it, and we ended up in a stupid argument."

"So you believe that if you confront him, you'll start an argument?" I asked, making sure I understood her fears.

She nodded. "But what else can I do?"

Mindy had to develop several different strategies for avoiding arguments with Mel. Increasing her internal locus of control (see page 43) would give her self-esteem. This would be an immediate boost because she'd quit blaming herself for *Mel's problem*. She agreed to use overt self-instruction to program the following thought into her mind: "I have the power to stop arguments by refusing to participate."

Extinction

Before giving her further instructions, I made certain that Mindy was in no danger of being physically abused. Once I understood that *she* knew she was safe from harm, I suggested she use *extinction*, a simple confrontation technique, to cope with Mel's temper while she was developing an "internal" attitude. (Had she feared for her physical safety, Mindy would have had an entirely different problem—one calling for a more intensive intervention.)

Extinction is the psychological term for totally ignoring another person's behavior. Research has concluded that when behavior is ignored, a person will eventually reduce its occurences. The behavior "extinguishes."

If you decide to extinguish an argument, say absolutely nothing in reaction to your man's first inflammatory remark. Turn away and return to what you were doing, or start doing something else. In Mindy's case, when Mel said, "Can't you handle anything?" the extinction technique would have demanded that Mindy turn around and walk away *without saying one word or uttering a sound.*

"He'd get furious," Mindy said, obviously worried about the aftermath of extinction.

"That could very well be. Research suggests that when one person extinguishes another person's behavior, the other person may temporarily increase his or her behavior in an effort to get attention. If Mel does get furious, it will indicate that he doesn't want to be extinguished, that he wants you to engage in the old habit."

"I thought you said your recommendations wouldn't make things worse?"

"If his being furious makes things worse for you," I explained supportively, "stop doing the technique immediately. Confrontation is supposed to give you strength, not cause you problems. If you walk away and absolutely can't stand his anger, then walk back into the room and remind him of what you're trying to do."

I strongly advise you to find a peaceful moment to explain extinction to your man before ever using it. A few simple words work best. You might say, "I realize that you get upset, but arguing only hurts us and I don't want to do it anymore. When things heat up, the best thing for me to do is walk away from the situation and then start over again in a few minutes."

At the first sign of an argument, walk out of the room, take some deep breaths, and calm down for five minutes. When you've regained your composure, walk back into the room and try to engage your man in a casual conversation. Tell him about something that happened that day. You can talk about the issue that triggered his remarks after you've reestablished lines of communication.

Another problem that makes extinction difficult is the fact that many men refuse to extinguish. That is, if you walk out of the room, he may follow you. If that happens, then you know your extinction has caused him to realize that he's the one who's out of control; and he won't like that. Getting you to argue will help him regain a sense of control, however irrational that may sound.

Though extinction seems passive, it's actually confrontational in nature. Doing nothing when your man hits your "arguing button" is a statement of assertiveness and strength. It's also a technique that conserves psychological energy. When a woman like Mindy becomes worn out from running a house, supervising two kids, and dealing with her own unmet needs, she must use a technique that gives her a maximum chance of success with a minimum of effort.

Extinction will automatically make things better for you, if for no other reason than the fact that it will help you avoid the pain and frustration of an argument. If your man cooperates with you, your actions can lead to a discussion of how you feel when his temper flares, how he can get your attention without starting an argument, and how your walking away is actually a statement of love for him.

Extinction has a dual purpose. It provides a rational alternative to take *at the very moment* a problem surfaces, and it breaks the typical chain of events, causing your man to say, "What's going on here?" *This is* when you will have his attention and he will be able to hear what you say. In Mindy's case, what she will say when Mel asks her why she walked away will be more important than the act of walking away itself.

As is the case with most confrontations, extinction has its down side. That is, you could use it to dismiss your man when he's trying to confront you about a problem he sees in you. If he confronts you in a rational manner about your excessive spending or your bitterness and you walk away, you are misusing extinction. Remember: just because you're helping your man learn to love you better doesn't mean you've quit being a fallible human being yourself.

You can avoid using extinction inappropriately by always returning to a conversation and trying to discuss the topic without personal attack. If that doesn't work, you can always walk away again.

Before discussing another technique for coping with your man's temper, I want to remind you of the most important guideline for this or any confrontation. If you are bothered or afraid of extinction—no matter what the reason—abandon it immediately. There's always something else you can do. You are your own best therapist; don't let me or anyone else take that away from you.

Cognitive Modeling

If you don't like extinction or your man doesn't extinguish very well, you might try a more sophisticated strategy: *cognitive modeling.*

Cognitive modeling will permit you to assert yourself both verbally and creatively. It has a greater chance of stimulating a change in your man's behavior; it also requires more energy and some practice. The most promising thing about this technique is that it interrupts your man's temper tantrum in such a way that he may regain control.

The most important aspect of cognitive modeling is the breaking of eye contact with your man. When eye contact is broken, the momentum that often propels arguing is lessened. When using cognitive modeling, intentionally turn away from face-to-face contact with your man and let him hear what's going on inside your head. In a calm tone, verbalize your feelings and then think aloud about what can be done to solve the problem.

"This is how it might work," I explained to Mindy. "Let's say you're standing in the kitchen when Mel comes in and he starts to complain about the noisy dishwasher. At first you say nothing, but he continues to complain. Finally you turn your head twenty degrees away from him, pretend that the refrigerator is your best friend, and say, 'I'm really beginning to resent Mel for always picking on me. Why can't we just talk normally about what's bothering him? Anything I say only makes matters worse. I don't know what to do. I feel so incompetent and confused.'

"Then turn back to Mel, repeat your final thought, and make a request: 'Could you please just try to tell me what's bothering you?' "

Don't attack your man during cognitive modeling. When you think aloud, be careful not to condemn, analyze, or patronize him. Verbalize your feelings of frustration, and if anything, criticize yourself. Emphasize the mutuality of your problem by using *we* instead of *him* or *you*.

If cognitive modeling doesn't work for you, or if you find it awkward, embarrassing, or frightening for any reason, drop it immediately. There are other things you can do. (Remember that you can adapt any one of my programs to any problem you think it might fit. Let your creativity and my guidelines direct your effort.)

Stimulus-Control Program

There's one other technique you can use to avoid an argument. It was a godsend for Cathy.

"Bob gets home around six at night," Cathy explained. "And I usually get home about twenty minutes before him. I'm right in the middle of dealing with two wild kids, getting the mail, answering the phone, and preparing food when he walks in the house with a chip on his shoulder and immediately starts criticizing me for something I've done or not done.

"He'll blurt out some curse word, and then ask me why Kevin's plastic turtle is sitting in the front yard, or how could I let the neighbor boy do such a lousy job cutting the grass. I try to help him relax, but we always end up arguing."

Bob's groundless accusation was usually the last straw in Cathy's stress-filled day. Her role as an executive assistant was rewarding but demanding. It took so much of her time and energy that she often felt inadequate as a mother and homemaker. By the time Bob walked in the door, she needed his support as much as he needed hers. Cathy was too tired to implement extinction or cognitive modeling. That's why I recommended the *stimulus-control program*. In short, this program advises, "Sometimes you have to say 'I surrender.' "

When you use this program, you're admitting that once a certain troublesome situation begins, you're unable to control your reaction to it. The key to stimulus control is to institute an avoidance program far enough ahead of time so that the troublesome situation never has a chance to develop. While you can't control your man's mind or his mood, you *can* control the situation that typically gives rise to an argument.

Five or ten minutes before the critical moment is sure to occur (that's the *stimulus* you're controlling), take your kids and run a short errand. Go to the grocery store and pick up a gallon of milk. You only have to be gone long enough for the situation, and hence the critical moment, to pass.

When your man asks you where you've been, tell him the truth. Tell him that you're unable to control your reaction to the troublesome situation. You might say, "I'm unable to deal with your anger when you get home, so I decided to avoid the situation." And you might wish to add, "I think we need to discuss this so I don't feel like I'm being chased out of my own home."

If the stimulus-control program is successful, there's a chance your man will implement a control program of his own. No man should be ashamed to admit he's unable to come straight home from work without "dumping" his stress on his family. He could control the situation by stopping by the health club for a short workout. (Stopping by the bar for a couple of beers increases, rather than decreases, stress.)

While it's true that stimulus control does not resolve the original problem, it does avoid adding stress to a stressful situation. It can also encourage both parties to rationally investigate the cause of the tension. It's a stopgap measure that can lead to solving problems by not creating any new ones.

When He Sulks Like a Little Boy

Cathy brought up a dimension of bad temper that Mindy didn't have to face. "There's a good chance," she said, "that if I tell Bob why I left, he'll spend the rest of the evening sulking."

"What do you mean, 'sulking'?"

"He won't talk during dinner," Cathy replied with exasperation in her voice, "and he'll sit around the rest of the night watching television with a hurt look on his face."

Sulking is an example of passive aggressiveness, like the four-year-old who threatens to hold his breath until he gets a cookie. It's aggressive because it's hostile and manipulative; it's passive because the sulker doesn't say or do anything. This makes sulking more difficult to cope with than an actual outburst of anger.

Sulking is particularly difficult for a woman to cope with because the childish nature of the action stimulates her mothering response. Before she knows it, she's saying something to cheer him up, to lecture him, or to admonish him as if she were dealing with a child. However, no matter what she says or does, she ends up paying attention to the sulker and encouraging him to continue his sulking. That's why the best way to deal with sulking is to ignore it.

"You mean," Cathy said, obviously frustrated, "that you want me to let him spoil my evening by making me watch a grown man behave like a little boy?"

"The first few evenings of ignoring probably *will* be spoiled," I replied. "Your only other alternative is to give in to his tantrum, pay attention to him, and thereby encourage him to do it again. You must redirect your nurturing response by realizing that ignoring Bob's sulks is the only real way to help him. In effect, you say, 'I won't dignify your sulking by responding.' "

"Knowing me, I'll have to say *something*."

If you're like Cathy and feel you *have* to say something in reaction to your man's sulking, use *rational anger* to confront him.

Rational anger is the controlled expression of anger for the purpose of gaining your man's attention. It gives you a chance to voice your frustration in a constructive manner. In other words, you'd be saying to him, "I'm angry, so pay attention to what I'm saying."

Rational anger embodies a confrontation that's somewhere between a simple act of assertiveness and an angry outburst. An example of anger spoken rationally might be, "I don't want to have to watch your damn sulking again!"

If you use rational anger to express your frustrations, expect your heart to pound and your voice to crack. If your anger stimulates a rational conversation, be prepared to calmly discuss your concerns. If his sulking continues (which is most likely), you have no alternative but to walk out of the room and ignore him.

If you have a man who sulks, I'm sure you've tried to draw him out by asking a leading question. For example, "Are you going to mow the lawn tomorrow?" If he's like most sulkers, he'll grunt and draw deeper within himself. Once you have your own frustration under control, you might try asking him a more general question. For example, "Is there anything I can do to help?" He'll probably just sigh and say no. But such a question will make it easier for you to walk away.

When He Holds His Anger Inside

"I think he's afraid to get mad at me," Nancy, a thirty-year-old flight attendant, told me. "Is that possible?"

"It's very possible," I answered. "But it's also possible that you're protecting him from his anger. Perhaps that tendency is one of the occupational hazards of being a stewardess."

"Well," she explained softly, "when Carl gets mad at me, he doesn't say a word, but I can see it on his face. I wish he could just say whatever's on his mind. But he holds it inside and we never get to talk it out. It takes two or three days before things return to normal, if they ever do. We seem to be growing apart."

When a man gets angry at the woman he loves, he often experiences an instantaneous fear. He says to himself, "Something terrible will happen if I get angry at my woman." I expect that this fear is caused by a male protective instinct, which, incidentally, is just as strong as a woman's mothering instinct. The resultant emotional state is similar to panic, so it's not surprising that outwardly he appears to freeze.

A woman rarely has the objectivity to understand this complicated maze of psychological events, and she reacts with her own instinct—she nurtures. In doing so, she unintentionally gives her man even more reason to feel bad, because he begins to think, "I'm being so unreasonable and she's still being nice to me. She really ought to be nasty—that's what I deserve."

I told Nancy I thought that Carl might even get a strange sense of enjoyment out of her getting mad at him.

"He does!" Nancy exclaimed. "I've never understood why he got this smirk on his face when I finally blew up at him. Now you're telling me that he's smiling because he's happy to get what he thinks he deserves."

"Exactly."

"Well maybe I should just get mad at him more often," she exclaimed, somewhat sarcastically.

"Many women do that, but it only leads to more estrangement, because the man never faces his fear and learns to express his anger."

Nancy's goal was to be as strong and as self-possessed as she possibly could be. I suggested she implement the *self-critique hierarchy*, a long-term program with three distinct objectives: to help her become more of an "internal" woman; to enable her to confront her tendency to protect her husband from his anger; and, indirectly, to help Carl learn to face himself. The program works as follows.

When criticizing yourself, avoid sarcasm and self-pity. Be honest, yet feel free to avoid any area that causes you discomfort. The reason I call it a hierarchy is that you begin the self-critique with a simple criticism. If that feels comfortable, the criticism becomes more complicated and begins to involve your man.

It may seem strange that criticizing yourself will help your man express *his* anger. The rationale is this: with the self-critique hierarchy, you demonstrate that honest self-criticism is a strength. If he's paying attention, there's a good chance he will hear how intimately he's involved in your life. This will encourage him to follow your lead and be honest with you about his own weaknesses, most especially his fear of his own anger.

If you're uncertain whether or not to criticize yourself in front of your man, you can practice the program by telling a coworker how stupid you felt when you misread the time and missed the train. Or confide in a casual acquaintance how disappointed you were in yourself for becoming unduly upset with a store clerk. You can practice the self-critique program as much as you wish. It certainly won't hurt to increase your skills of honest self-criticism.

I reminded Nancy to progress slowly in the program so that she wouldn't overexpose herself. If she revealed too many weaknesses without any indication that Carl would reciprocate, she could end up hurting herself.

I suggested a five-step hierarchy and then helped Nancy develop some actual words to use that were relevant to a recent troublesome visit by Carl's parents. In typical fashion, Carl's mother had criticized everything while his father remained silent.

1. Identify a Hope That Went Awry.

"I wanted things to go so well. Maybe I was a bit too unrealistic, given the problems we've had in the past."

2. Identify an Excess in Your Attitude.

"I could feel myself trying too hard to please everyone at once. I should have known it would backfire."

3. Share a Problem.

"I get so mad at Cindy's disrespect I can't see straight. I never knew a daughter could be so disrespectful to her mother. I know I'm the adult, but gosh, teenagers can drive you crazy."

4. Become a Bit More Personal.

"I get so mad at your father when he treats you so coldly even though you'd give anything for a little praise."

5. Be as Direct as Possible.

"I know I overreact, but I see you standing on your head to please him, and then I get the fallout of your frustration."

You may implement the self-critique hierarchy over a period of days, hours, or even within the same conversation. Move on to the next, more intimate, and possibly more confrontational self-criticism when your man indicates his readiness. For example, if he gets defensive at one level, don't move on until he can talk to you about his reaction. If he adds his *own* criticism of you to your self-critique, suspend the program.

Remember: the primary goal of the self-critique program is for you to gain enough strength so that you no longer protect your man from constructive criticism. The secondary goal is for your man to begin his own program of self-criticism. Your best chance of achieving this secondary goal occurs when you rationally explain the program to him. The self-critique hierarchy is one of those programs that has a major impact on your relationship if it works, but it also has a good chance of not working.

Sometimes You Have to Call Time Out

If you get tired or frustrated when coping with his temper, suggest to your man that you both implement a one-day program called *pleasuring*. During pleasuring, both partners agree not to discuss any topic that engenders arguments and to avoid making any difficult decisions unless absolutely necessary.

I tell couples to remember the romantic phase of their relationship and to recall the little pleasures that each likes. These should be nonverbal and should involve gentle touching of nonsexual parts of the body, for example, rubbing toes, massaging the scalp or back, and combing hair. During pleasuring, all unnecessary attempts to solve problems should be extinguished by one partner's calling time out and the other partner quickly complying.

Like most of my techniques, this program has limited application if your man refuses to participate. It does, after all, take two people to please each other, just as it takes two to fight. It's one of those things about love that there's just no getting around.

9.

OVERCOMING WORK INTERFERENCE

Cindy, a part-time clerk and full-time homemaker and mother, summarized her complaint this way: "Charlie is a wonderful provider, but I think he's being unfair to me. I know he disagrees with me, but he's always bringing his work home with him. I feel as if I come second to his work."

Charlie's dedication to work and to making money had forced his love life into a secondary position. Disagreements with Cindy over the relative importance of work and family reflected the conflict in their priorities. Cindy believed that Charlie's obsession with his life at the office was a sign that he didn't respect her homemaker role. He, on the other hand, complained that she simply didn't understand how hard he had to work.

Although Charlie came with Cindy to two counseling sessions, he was still reluctant to admit that his work interfered with his love relationship. Their argument over the stress his job caused at home was endless. Cindy believed that love must be based on intimacy, while Charlie felt he had to keep his eye on the checkbook. Love versus money . . . a conflict as old as love itself, but one that must be resolved if love is to thrive. However, Charlie showed no willingness to compromise.

When He Won't Compromise

Priorities Checklist

I gave Cindy the *priorities checklist,* which helped her determine the relative importance of work and love within her relationship. It also gave her a safe way to confront Charlie's preoccupation with work.

If you work with the checklist first, show your results to your man, and explain exactly what you're doing, there's an excellent chance that he, too, will work with it. If he doesn't, ask him for his reaction to your results. The checklist is an excellent way to structure a conversation without enduring all the hassles that follow the ominous-sounding, "We have to talk, Charlie."

I've ranked ten behaviors in ascending order of importance. Make the checklist work for you by realigning my ranking in keeping with your values. Then share the list with your man, encouraging him to rank it according to *his* values. You should both feel free to delete items you consider less relevant to your life style and to add items that you consider more important.

1. Doing household chores
2. Telling my partner, "Thanks for your help"
3. Initiating stimulating conversation
4. Disclosing private feelings
5. Supporting each other's career (including homemaking)
6. Choosing to be with my partner rather than with friends
7. Being sensitive to my partner's sexual needs
8. Bringing home money
9. Being involved with the kids
10. Being sensitive to my partner's emotional needs

When Cindy showed her list to Charlie, he couldn't resist making one of his own. Initially, he wanted to argue about the differences between their lists, but Cindy refused, telling him, "I'd love to discuss our differences, but I will not fight about them."

Cindy gave "Bringing home money" a priority ranking of 3, and "Doing household chores" a 6. Charlie ranked "Bringing home money" at 9 and "Supporting each other's career" at 10. Adapting the list to their own relationship, Cindy added "Stopping arguments" at position 7, and Charlie added "Spending money wisely" at position 8.

Since there was no scoring of the checklist, Cindy and Charlie were able to use it to improve their mutual understanding with a minimum of arguing. Charlie had never realized that helping around the house was so important to Cindy; and Cindy had never understood how Charlie really felt about her spending habits.

Many couples are not as fortunate as Cindy and Charlie. A lot of men can't see beyond their belief that making a lot of money absolves them of their responsibility to the family. These men don't often give themselves the right to relax and have fun. Consequently, they don't know how to do anything but work. But since they don't admit their shortcoming, they never learn how to reduce the stress that their job places on their family. Consequently, they don't enjoy the warmth and peace that their hard work could bring.

Many of the women react to this frustrating situation by making general complaints that only add to the confusion. Phrases like "unfair to the rest of the family," "brings his work home with him," and "shuts me out of his life" don't really communicate the real issues at hand.

It may take several attempts at ranking the priorities checklist before the gap can be lessened between your desire for more love and his desire for more money. But the gap must be closed, and he must do much of the work. The analytical nature of the checklist makes it a little easier for him to translate his feelings for you into action. While he's grappling with the money/love issue, you can use the next technique to help him along.

Denominalization

When men are unable or unwilling to recognize how their work interferes with their family, I recommend that women use the *denominalization program.* Denominalization means to state your complaints in clear, precise language, ridding your speech of ambiguity.

Most women probably know what their complaints mean in terms of situations and behaviors, but their men don't. Women are surprised to learn that their men don't know the answer to the question, "What exactly must you do or say to help your wife with her frustrations?" A woman can increase her man's understanding by translating her wishes—being "fair," "leaving your work at the office," and "opening your life to me"—into specific requests. Here's how denominalization worked in Cindy's case.

Instead of complaining that he wasn't fair, she asked her husband to spend every Saturday and Sunday afternoon doing something with her and the kids. Rather than telling him to leave his work at the office, she requested that he listen to her talk about her day twice as long as he complained about his work problems. And instead of saying that he shuts her out of his life, she encouraged him to ask her opinion about work problems or share with her how he felt during a stressful meeting.

You can further emphasize the need for specificity by seeking clarification from your man when he voices a complaint. Use the techniques of active listening and passive questioning to translate that complaint into a specific request. Begin by rephrasing his complaint. For example, you might say, "I think I heard you say that you get uptight when I gossip with my friends about other people." Then use a question to help him translate his complaint into a request for specific action. "Would it help if I tried my best not to gossip when you might hear it?"

There are two drawbacks to denominalization. Once you've translated your complaints into specific requests, you face the possibility that your man will not meet them. This lack of cooperation can result in even more painful feelings of rejection. Second, specifying your needs may bring you face to face with your own feelings of inferiority. You may not think you're a good enough person to receive such specific consideration. However, both of these drawbacks, if worked through via other programs (for example, self-acceptance), can result in a much improved love relationship.

When You Need Help Around the House

"I need help around the house," is a major complaint of women whose man won't change. Though many men will logically agree that their wives need help around the house, the attitude that housework is women's work can be so deeply ingrained that they will unconsciously refuse to follow through.

Part of the reason your man "forgets" to help you around the house is that you go along with it. If you're a working mother, your guilt about leaving your child with a baby-sitter weakens your assertiveness. You don't feel you have a right to ask for help. Many women who work outside the home cope with the guilt by intensifying their childcare behavior when they are home.

Househusband-Shaping Program

The findings of one research study might possibly solve several of your problems at once. The study's most critical conclusion is this: fathers who take care of their kids begin to do more household tasks.

Use this finding to implement the *househusband-shaping program.* The guidelines are as follows: realize that your mothering response may be excessive and that you need to curtail it; reduce the number of basic childcare tasks you do for your child(ren); ask your man to do them instead.

Explain the research finding to your man so that he won't think you're trying to brainwash him. Tell him that if he begins to do a few simple childcare tasks (cooking hotdogs, picking up after the kids, reading them a story), there is every reason to believe that he will be like the men in the research study; that is, he will begin to do household chores as an automatic extension of his childcare behavior. This will help him feel better about keeping his promise.

Another important bit of information to communicate to your man is this: children raised under conditions in which Dad does household chores have significantly less restrictive stereotypes about the roles of men and women and a much better chance of having a rewarding love relationship.

Another complication in getting your man to help you around

the house is that he may not want you to work in the first place.

Rising rates of divorce, delinquency, male impotency, and illegitimacy have, from time to time, been blamed on the working woman. But at a time when 3 out of 5 working women have preschoolers at home, it is worthwhile to consider this conclusion from another research report: *the fact that a woman works outside of the home appears to have no direct impact on the success of her love relationship or health of her children.*

My clinical experience supports this conclusion. I've seen working women organize their lives so that they are just as efficient as full-time homemakers; I've helped homemakers who have so much time on their hands that they over-parent their children and mother their husbands. I'm acquainted with homemakers who are very happy being just exactly what they are; and I've counseled working women who are on the verge of a nervous breakdown. There's no simple cause-and-effect relationship between working women and troubles at home.

There does seem to be one guideline that the working woman can follow to reduce the likelihood of trouble: she should delete one role (laundress, full-time cook) from her repertoire of homemaking behaviors. The man, an older child, or hired help can be used to take up the slack.

If He Treats You Like an Enemy

Bob and Diane's work problem was slightly different from Cindy and Charlie's. Each considered himself or herself to be a career professional; Bob was a sales executive and Diane an advertising executive. They had one child, a twelve-year-old boy.

They often accused each other of being selfish, of not understanding the need of each for freedom from daily responsibilities, and of not being supportive. The fact that Diane attended evening meetings and Bob often traveled overnight during the week made problem-solving especially difficult. Bob didn't want to talk about their conflict with a professional counselor; he didn't think they had a big problem. But Diane's nerves were becoming more and more frazzled. She took the initiative.

Working Couples' Management Plan

"You need to implement a management program," I told her. "The one I like best is called *the working couples' management plan.* Of course, I encourage you to explain the plan to Bob, but you needn't wait for his full cooperation before implementing it."

I suggested to Diane that she first review the four categories working couples typically fall into and see where she and Bob fit. These categories are:

ADVERSARIES. Both partners are highly involved in their respective careers and only minimally involved at home. There's a lot of conflict over household responsibilities. Each person wants a majority of support from the other. Children represent a major source of disagreement and stress.

ACCOMMODATOR. One partner is highly career-oriented (usually the man) while the other (usually the woman) focuses on the home and family. The career partner often falls into the trap of thinking that his or her role is more important than the other partner's. The household partner can easily begin to resent playing the accommodator role.

ALLIES. Both partners share an involvement in either their careers or their home life. If they emphasize careers, then neither worries about having an organized home; if home is most important, they focus on helping each other reduce the impact of job stress on the family. One or both of the partners may suppress a complaint in order not to create stress.

ACROBATS. Both partners try to do everything to perfection—high career achievement, supportive relationship, happy children, organized home, excellent socialization, etc. Exhaustion and reduced sexual relationships are two frequent side effects of this category. Women have a harder time letting go of the acrobat role than men do.

It took Diane only seconds to realize that she and Bob acted as adversaries.

"How do I get him to become my ally," she asked sincerely, "if he doesn't think we have a serious problem."

"Why don't you begin to act as his ally and see if he reciprocates," I suggested.

"I've already tried that, and he still refuses to see my point of view."

"Then back up even farther and become your own ally."

"What do you mean?"

"Don't try so hard to keep your house clean and have dinner ready every night. Do your best, and if something is messy, the heck with it; shove it in a corner until later."

Diane was ambivalent about my recommendation. On the one hand, she was relieved at the thought that it was okay if her home wasn't the neatest. On the other, she felt guilty.

"I've always thought I should have a neat and tidy home like my mother did," Diane said. "But it's so obvious that Mom spent a lot of time on the house. I haven't got that time. I never thought I'd say it, but maybe I'll hire someone to clean once a week."

"And you know," I said, "it won't kill that preteen of yours to have a few chores. Tell him if he doesn't do them, he doesn't get any money; either that or he loses a privilege."

Here are some other guidelines I gave to Diane in the hope that she would become her own ally and bring Bob around to her way of thinking. Apply them to your situation.

- *Guard personal time.* Find ways of spending some time pursuing personal goals. In Diane's case, she needed to take more time to disengage from her job at the end of the day. She had trouble rediscovering all the things she liked about her femininity once her work day was over. She needed to listen to music, take a bubble bath, or buy new lingerie in order to get back into this role.

  Any little thing you can do to make that transition will reduce your stress and give you more energy to confront the needs of your relationship.

- *Ask for support.* Many partners think they are being selfish if they ask for support. If you have a loving relationship, your partner wants and needs the opportunity to help you, even if that means just listening to your complaints. I told Diane to simply ask Bob to rub her neck, put a romantic song on the stereo, or give her a lingering kiss without expecting her to have sex. (See the ten-second kiss rule, page 122). Then she should be alone for thirty minutes and nurture herself.
- *Limit outside obligations.* If one or both partners make too many commitments to social and community projects, there won't be enough time to nurture the relationship.
- *Get away.* Each couple should have an activity that will take them away from stress. A weekend in the country, a day at the flea market, a week on the beach, and a few days at a friend's house all represent opportunities to "get away from it all."
- *Back-up for sick kids.* If they have children, dual-career couples should develop one or two reliable resources they can call upon at the last minute to cover for a sick child.

"I don't understand how this plan will reduce the pressure on *me*," Diane said. "It sounds as if it will decrease Bob's pressure but increase mine."

"Maybe I didn't make it clear enough," I said. "When implemented without the full cooperation of your partner, this plan still requires that you drop one of your household roles. Ideally, Bob should pick up that role or you should hire someone to do it. I thought we agreed that you'd drop the house-cleaning role and hire someone to take it over, or at least severely curtail it."

"But what should I do when I can't stand how messy the house has become?" Diane asked.

"Clean. Just don't clean because you think you *should*, or because your mother would be mad if you didn't, or for any other compulsive reason. Clean because it makes you feel better.

"Also, whenever possible, increase your and Bob's *companionate activity*," I said, introducing a strategy that all couples should implement. "Run errands together, or meet for lunch, or simply

111

take a walk. The very act of being together has been shown to offset the stress of struggling to make a relationship work."

When He Forgets You're a Person and Treats You Like the Maid

"I'm a housewife and proud of it," thirty-eight-year-old Peggy said. It was obvious that this pert, toughened farm girl meant exactly what she said. "My husband says he respects my job, but he really doesn't know what it's like. My problem is that I never get to talk to adults. If I'm not doing something for my three kids, I'm watching a neighbor's child or doing something at school. The few times I talk to my girl friend, we talk about either her kids or mine.

"When Darryl comes home, he wants to see the kids or talk to me about my day around the house. I feel guilty if I say 'to hell with the house and kids.' I hate to complain, but I'm beginning to resent his freedom. He talks to adults all day long about adult things. He doesn't seem to understand that I need the same thing."

"I'm sure you tell him this," I said. "Don't you?"

"Sure I do." Peggy seemed trapped between her love for her family and her desire to have a life of her own. "But he tells me to get out of the house and get a job. He doesn't understand that I don't want to leave the kids and get a job. All I want is for him to pay attention to me as a person, not as the mother of his children or the keeper of his house."

Nonverbal Rapprochement

I felt that Peggy needed to "reintroduce" herself to her husband, using a technique called *nonverbal rapprochement*. It's such a soft and loving technique that it might not be seen as confrontational.

Like many of the programs presented in this book, nonverbal rapprochement operates on the law of human reciprocity. That is, there seems to be a built-in genetic code that causes humans to return kindness for kindness received. There are, of course, many things that can go wrong within this law. But as long as you don't expect your situation to change overnight, there's no reason not to try this approach.

The rapprochement is comprised of three nonverbal acts: touching, smiling, and head nods. To implement this technique, use any one or a combination of these whenever you're near your partner. For example, greet him with a smile and a soft touch when he comes in from work. Nod your head when you're looking at him and he's speaking. Sit beside him and rub his neck when he's talking to the kids. Smile at him when he looks at you.

If the law of reciprocity is working in your favor, your man will be moved to give back the kindness he's received. However, there can be some problems. He may take your nonverbal rapprochement as a sexual signal, which it may or may not be. If he questions you about your behavior, tell him the absolute truth—that by renewing your admiration for him, you hope that he will learn to appreciate you all over again.

You may be tempted to strategize your nonverbal acts as if there's a formula that will lead to success. This is not a surreptitious nor manipulative technique, used to control another without his knowledge. If you fall into this trap, you'll be acting with an external locus of control and it will get you into trouble.

Finally, research indicates that this technique will not work if there is considerable distress in your relationship.

One final reminder: when you use this or any other program of confrontation, your man will undoubtedly ask you what is going on. You should capitalize on this moment by clearly and precisely explaining your complaint and what you're doing to try and help your relationship. You have an excellent chance of being heard, even if he rarely listens to you.

10.

DEALING WITH SEXUAL PROBLEMS

When Your Sex Life Is Going Nowhere

It's often said that your most important sex organ is between your ears, not your legs. If your attitudes toward your body and inner self are negative, and your thoughts about him are cautious and apprehensive, your body isn't going to become sexually aroused.

Statistics indicate that over half of all serious relationships will experience some sexual problems. These problems range from a simple wish for improved foreplay to impotence and frigidity. My clinical experience suggests that the percentage is even higher. Whether married or not, if you face any kind of sexual problem, even if it seems to be your man's problem, I encourage you to complete the *sexual reevaluation program.*

Even if you don't have a sexual problem, this program will help you determine where your sex life is going, identify any problem areas, and guide you in deciding what, if any, changes to make.

114

The Sexual Reevaluation Program

The program has five steps:

1. STOP HAVING SEX. If your sex life is deteriorating—if you move from lover to lover with little satisfaction or sex with your man is more pain than gain—I recommend that you suspend all sexual activity with your man and give yourself time to relax. Use a bit of common wisdom to offset the disappointment you may feel: sex is perfectly natural, but rarely is it naturally perfect.

2. GATHER INFORMATION. I recommend a dose of the best of all possible treatments for sexual problems, if indeed you have one: information. Consider the following:

- Women are typically less aware of their own arousal than are men. This is probably due to the fact that women are usually held responsible for monitoring a man's arousal so that they won't get pregnant or be considered immoral. Many women are so busy policing their partner's sexual response that they don't have time to focus on their own.
- A "personality fit" with a sex partner is much more important to a woman than to a man.
- Sexually unresponsive women are often homemakers, socially inhibited, and restrictive in their attitudes toward life.
- Most women who report sexual satisfaction had a childhood home life in which there was little mother-daughter conflict; in which the father was present and active in discipline; in which the parents' marriage was loving; in which there was no older sister; and in which there was peace and order.
- Women who remember learning about the woman's role in reproduction first are usually more sexually satisfied than those who were first told about a man's role.
- Women who have regular orgasms have a more positive attitude toward masturbation than woman with irregular orgasms.
- Physical attributes such as weight, breast size, size of clitoris,

115

and attractiveness do not correlate with consistency of female sexual orgasm. Nor do such things as the mother's sexual attitudes or history, frequency of menstruation, pregnancy, factors associated with the first sex act, craving for extramarital affairs, or frequency of masturbation.

Avoid situations in which you find yourself policing a man's sexual arousal. Don't apologize for an attitude that says, "I need to get to know you before we can have sex."

3. ANALYZE YOUR SEX GUILT. Complete a *sex-guilt analysis*, an exercise that will eventually help you confront any man who tries to take sexual advantage of you. (Marriage does not protect a woman from sexual exploitation).

Begin the analysis by searching your memory for sexual experiences and asking, "How much guilt do I have about my sexuality?" If you're like many women, you have a considerable amount of sex guilt. Sex guilt is expressed in such feelings as, "I shouldn't have enjoyed intercourse with that guy," "Wanting oral sex makes me a bad person," and "I can't stop feeling bad about having sex with the wrong person."

Next, review your morality regarding sexuality. If your sex guilt is intense, then your morality may verge on fanaticism. The voice of excessive morality often masks sexual guilt, and sounds like this: "Oral sex is a dirty, awful sin," "Women should never let on that they enjoy sex," and, "Women must control their lustful, animal instincts."

If you have both sex guilt and an excessive sexual morality, you are trapped; that is, sex guilt prohibits you from freely evaluating your sexual experiences as it reinforces excessive sexual morality. Without a rational sexual morality, it's nearly impossible to avoid making mistakes and feeling guilty.

Researchers have found that high-guilt, excessive-morality women are more gullible to the "lines" men sometimes use for seduction purposes. Conversely, women with low sex guilt have a more rational sense of sexual morality and are much less likely to be taken advantage of. You are well-advised to eliminate sex guilt by accepting yourself as a sexual creature (see Chapter 2) and putting your morality in proper perspective.

Sexual sophistication is not a measure of how many men you've slept with or how many orgasms you can have in an hour. In truth, it's a measure of how free you are to examine your conscience and make informed decisions about what you want to do with *your* body.

4. RESTRUCTURE YOUR SEXUAL ATTITUDES. This will take time, but you can begin immediately by reprogramming your brain with these two attitudes: "I have a right to enjoy my body," and, "My morality must work for, not against, me." If repeated several times a day, these and similar self-instructions can lead to an unrestricted evaluation of your sexual experiences, to a refinement of your moral reasoning, and to a significant reduction of guilt.

5. CHANGE NEGATIVE AUTOMATIC THOUGHTS. Examine yourself carefully for thoughts that may be contributing to your self-abuse. That's right! Many women who complain that men take advantage of them sexually, actually abuse *themselves* with unrealistic attitudes.

Research suggests that perfectionist thinking is a major contributor to sexual dysfunction. This thinking, in the form of automatic thoughts, occurs before, during, and after sex. Identify the automatic thoughts that are interfering with your sex life. Which of the following thoughts are going through your mind *before* sex?

> I have to be in control.
> I have to please him.
> I have to enjoy it.
> It'll be terrible if I don't perform.
> I couldn't ask for that.
> He won't like it if I do it.
> It's not nice to do that.
> What will he think of me?

These thoughts take you away from the enjoyment of your sexuality and into the confused world of rejection. Continue your evaluation of automatic thoughts by identifying those thoughts that may be occurring *during* sex.

> I don't think I'm becoming aroused.
> I haven't come yet . . . I probably won't.
> I'm naked but he's not excited . . . I'm not attractive.
> I'm not orgasmic . . . I'm not a real woman.

Needless to say, these thoughts exacerbate the fear of rejection as they increase sexual dysfunction. The next group of thoughts occurs after sex in women who are taking advantage of themselves. See if any of the following reflect your thoughts *after* sex.

> How awful this is!
> What a jerk I am!
> I shouldn't have to suffer this.
> God, he will hate me!
> I'm sure he'll never come back.

In addition to perfectionism, persons flooded with these automatic thoughts have an enormous need for approval, tend to avoid problems excessively, and take action to solve problems only when prompted by rising frustration. Their sexual dysfunction is just part of their overall unhappiness with life.

Once you've identified an automatic thought that's interfering with your sexual satisfaction, counter it by using overt self-instruction (see page 38) to give your brain a new, more rational thought. For example, if the thought is, "I have to please him," practice saying, "I want to please him and I know I can learn how." If the thought is, "I'm not a real woman," counter it with, "I can always be a real woman with a real man."

Once you've suspended your abusive automatic thoughts or learned how to identify and control them, you'll know where your problems end and his begin. Now you're ready to use the *sexual revitalization program* to help you and your man toward a more satisfactory sex life.

If lovers lack tenderness and intimacy, their sex life will suffer. As a result of the mad pursuit of the perfect orgasm, many lovers have lost sight of the fact that sex is the dessert of human interaction, not the main course.

Our Sex Life Is Lousy

"I know Jerry is discouraged with our sex life," Jo Ann said, "but he'll never come out and admit it. I'm going to have to confront the problem for both of us."

"Have you talked with anyone else about this?" I asked.

"Just my best friend, and my doctor. He said that Jerry and I should talk to a sex counselor, but I just can't imagine Jerry ever doing that. Anyhow, I don't want to talk about it, I just want a plan of action."

"You must know that talking about a sex problem can be very important if you want to correct it," I said, sensing her impatience.

Jo Ann nodded, but made it clear that she wanted to do something *now.* "I also know," she said hurriedly, "that talking isn't going to solve his impotence or my frustration. When I say action, Dr. Dan, that's exactly what I want!"

Jerry and Jo Ann were both thirty-five; they had two children, good jobs, and a lousy sex life. Jo Ann assured me that she and Jerry had a solid relationship and that the sex problem was more a result of their strict religious upbringing than a serious marital problem. Although I didn't approve of Jerry's not coming to counseling, Jo Ann insisted that he would respond if she guided him. I reasoned that if Jerry loved Jo Ann half as much as she obviously loved him, then there was a good chance that my self-management recommendations would work.

Jerry and Jo Ann were not that different from many couples. Jerry had moments of impotence, often induced by feelings of isolation and loneliness. Jo Ann endured her own moments of sexual frustration, and her passion was cooled by the psychological distance between her and her man. Both wanted a better sex life. But because of her willingness to face the facts, Jo Ann would have to be the one to get the ball rolling.

The Sexual Revitalization Program

The sexual revitalization program is a ten-step plan of action any woman can use to start her and her man on a path of rediscovering good sex. If you decide to adapt this outline to your situation, obviously your man must participate with you. If he refuses, then you'll be forced to consider the possibility that your love life is in serious jeopardy. (Chapter 16 will help.) However, if the program is only marginally successful, it's still possible that it will give your man enough confidence to accompany you to a sex therapist.

Here are the ten steps of the sexual revitalization program. They apply to both you and your man.

- Suspend all attempts at sexual intercourse. The simple act of not trying to have sex can relieve tension, making it easier to implement the other steps.
- Print a card for the mirror that says, "I have the right to have a sexual problem." Repeat this statement aloud but in private at least ten times a day. Make certain that the children do not read or hear this self-instruction.
- Consult your family doctor if there is any indication that the problem might be physical as well as mental (impotence can be treated medically).
- Use the programs outlined in Chapter 6, Improving Communication, to double-check your relationship for clear and concise communication. Also, implement one of the Games Lovers Can Play that you'll find in the next chapter, "Increasing Compatibility."
- Make a list of the automatic thoughts that are associated with your sexual dysfunction. (See the recommendations in the last section.) Read the list once a day for two weeks, each time focusing on the one(s) that apply to you. Your man should adapt the list to himself.

- Once you've identified one or two automatic thoughts that seem to give you the most trouble, reword them so that the threat is gone. This technique is called *decatastrophizing*. If you decatastrophize the thought, "What if I don't have an orgasm or have one too soon?" it becomes, "It's not terrible if I don't have an orgasm, I'll have plenty of chances in the future." Repeat the decatastrophized thought at least ten times a day. You'll note that decatastrophizing is a specialized form of cognitive restructuring.
- Read. Even with all of the advances in sex education, the primary treatment for sexual dysfunction is still information. You should be reading a good sex-education book regularly. I recommend *Dr. Ruth's Guide to Good Sex* by Dr. Ruth Westheimer and *Masters and Johnson On Sex and Human Loving* by Masters, Johnson, and Kolodny. Consider what you read carefully. You need to recognize and dispell the myths about sexuality.
- Look, touch, and tease. In a relaxed atmosphere, lie nude with your partner, looking at and touching each other's body in a nonsexual manner. Since many sexually dysfunctional persons have a negative view of their bodies, you can enhance your self-image by looking at and touching all parts of your *own* body, reminding yourself that your body is wonderful and should be appreciated.

As soon as you can look and touch without worrying about performing, begin the teasing technique. With your partner's help, practice gaining and losing full sexual arousal. If this proves too worrisome, do it by yourself at first.

- While relaxed, use your imagination to visualize the loss of arousal during intercourse. Practice self-acceptance (see page 38) and then decatastrophize the loss ("It's not terrible if I lose arousal"). After admitting your sexual fears to yourself, talk about them with your partner.
- If you and your partner encounter any failure during the program, take a deep breath and relax, hold hands, and

reassure each other that your sexual problems are merely bad habits of thinking and that you will eventually overcome them (provided medical causes have been ruled out).

If you have successful intercourse early in the program, do not be fooled into thinking the dysfunction has disappeared. Just because the organ between your legs worked, that doesn't mean that the more important organ between your ears won't give you any more trouble.

Provided you've moved slowly and confronted the situation in a loving manner, the sexual revitalization program should give you some relief within a few weeks. If not, you'll need to seek more intensive counseling.

A simple, passionate kiss can get you started on the sexual revitalization program. Tell your man that together you can make your sex life better by implementing the *ten-second kiss rule* at least twice a day. It's simple. You both agree that you'll kiss each other on the lips for at least 10 seconds twice a day, *without any direct genital stimulation*. During this kiss, both of you should concentrate on an image of your first passionate kiss together. After the kiss, comment on how good it felt and then change the subject. There's no sex allowed immediately following the ten-second kiss. This kiss rule will stimulate your desire and your affection, which, in turn, will put new passion into your sex life.

11.

INCREASING
COMPATIBILITY

Sometimes relationship distress is simply a matter of incompatibility. Dissimilar interests, divergent life styles, and differing moral viewpoints create a lack of harmony. A couple can begin a relationship thinking that they're compatible only to discover later on that they don't share the same fundamental ideas about life.

Here's how one woman summarized her confusion about the deterioration in her relationship.

"Jack and I have been married for four years," Linda said thoughtfully, "and I think our relationship might be in trouble. We just don't click like we used to. He goes out with the boys more often, our sex life has decreased, and we don't talk the way we should. I wanted him to come with me today, but he said that if I had a problem, I should go. I'm not really sure if the problem is me, him, or us."

When dealing with the issue of general compatibility, the problem is usually all three—you, him, and you (as a couple). However, in Jack and Linda's case, Jack carried more of the responsibility because he wouldn't even try to get help.

When He Won't Go to Counseling

Marriage counseling is a viable and important professional service. However, many professionals, in their mad dash for full appointment calendars, fail to tell us that although many couples could profit from professional counseling, they don't necessarily *need* it.

To determine whether you or your relationship needs professional help, you must conduct your own assessment. Using the "perfect partner traits" outlined on page 24, ask yourself: Am I grossly deficient in one or more of these traits? Is this deficiency causing me emotional suffering or otherwise interfering with the quality of my life? Have I tried my best to solve this problem? If you answer yes to these questions, you probably should seek individual counseling.

Then, ask of your relationship: Is there a specific problem I'd like to resolve? Have I tried to overcome this problem? Does there appear to be some type of obstacle between me and my partner? Have I tried self-help procedures (books, advice from a confidant)? Is the problem increasing my frustration? If you answered yes to these questions, then you probably should seek marriage counseling.

If you answered yes to both sets of questions, two or three hours of individual consultation will help you decide which type of counseling would be best for you. You might decide to seek both types.

If you do decide to seek counseling, get the names of three professionals from friends, other professionals, or the yellow pages. Call each one. After describing your problem briefly, ask, "Do you think you could help me with this?" and, "How do you work?" Do not expect the therapist to answer all your questions over the phone.

Make an appointment with the therapist you felt most comfortable with during the phone conversation. Tell your man what you're doing and why. If you want him to go with you (at first, you may not), ask him. If he says no, attend the first session yourself. If nothing else, use this session to determine whether or not you should be in counseling. Be careful: my experience has been that a majority of professionals—even reputable ones—tend to push people into counseling. Let me remind you once again: *your own best therapist is you.*

A competent therapist should smile and act warmly toward you, ask you questions about the specifics of your problem, demonstrate a knowledge and style that causes you to trust him or her, ask you for your opinion as to the cause of your problem, demonstrate a willingness to change his or her mind, and give you the feeling that he or she likes you and can help you.

If you decide to seek counseling, you should expect a clarification of your problem(s) and movement toward solving it *within four to six sessions.* If you don't see *some* movement in a fairly short period of time, find another therapist.

Therapist-Initiated Letter

At the beginning of my second session with Linda, she made it very clear that she wanted and needed marriage counseling and that Jack didn't want to come. I suggested that I write him a letter and explain the findings of a recent research report: in most cases, if one partner goes to marriage counseling without the other, the counseling itself can actually begin to contribute to the marital distress. This distress typically begins after the third visit.

Linda agreed to take my letter to Jack. Here is what I wrote:

Dear Jack,

As you know, your wife has sought help from me concerning her personal problems. Because we seem to be focusing on your marriage, I thought it was a good idea to brief you on a couple of things.

First, my approach to counseling is an educational one—I teach my "students" to be their own best therapists. I focus on specific situations and help the students improve their ability to solve problems. I do not blame one partner or take sides.

Second, research has shown that if one marital partner goes to counseling and talks about his or her marriage without the other partner present, those sessions themselves begin to contribute to marital distress somewhere around the third or fourth session. Therefore, in all good conscience, I cannot continue to talk to Linda about her marriage without you being present.

Please consider this letter carefully. Also, if you still decide not to come with Linda, would you please sign and return this letter? That way I'll know that you understand my concerns.

Sincerely,
Dr. Dan Kiley

If you're currently seeking help for a marital problem and your man refuses to attend the sessions, you should ask your counselor whether he or she will write a letter to your man. If the counselor agrees, explain what you read in this book about the therapist-initiated letter.

The letter should be straightforward, briefly explaining how the therapist conducts marital therapy, getting across the fact that one-spouse therapy eventually increases marital distress, and inviting the spouse to join in the sessions. At the bottom of the letter there should be a place for the spouse to sign. Once he or she has done so, the letter should be returned to the counselor.

One research study has reported that 68% of the spouses who received such a letter came to the next session. After Linda gave my letter to Jack, he started coming with her.

If your partner signs the letter and still won't go to counseling, your only avenue is to continue counseling and see what kind of personal growth you can accomplish on your own. Be aware that this recommendation may stimulate bitterness in you toward your man ("I'm doing all the work here"). If so, reread Chapter 4, Controlling Bitterness.

Marriage Encounter Weekend

Once Jack had made a commitment to counseling, Linda said, "I'm thinking of enrolling us in a marriage encounter weekend. What do you think?"

I gave Linda and Jack an overview of a marriage encounter weekend. "You spend two nights at a retreat house or motel.

Most of your time is structured by the following: prescribed time alone for reflection; writing your personal feelings on paper and then sharing them with your spouse; listening to professionals lecture on the characteristics of good marriages; spending time talking to each other about problems and solutions."

I also gave them the following results of a research project regarding marriage encounter weekends to help them make their own decision.

- Slightly more men than women (84% to 75%) thought the marriage encounter was helpful.
- More men than women (60% to 42%) are happier with their partner after the experience. (It is suggested that men liked the "homework" approach so prevalent in most encounter weekends. It seems easier for men to talk when they are told what they are to talk about and given a few words to begin.)
- Both men and women enjoyed the increase in communication, the time alone, and the overall improvement in their positive feelings toward the relationship.
- There's about a 10% chance that the exercise will have a lasting *negative* effect on your relationship. This comes from the fact that frustrating problems are aired but that the discussion does not lead to action.
- In most cases, there is little if any follow-up consultation.
- My own clinical experience with marriage encounter weekends has been mixed. Many partners have extolled their virtues, some have detested the experience, while others have seemed indifferent.

"The only clinical advice I can give you," I told Linda and Jack, "is that before enrolling in the marriage encounter weekend, you should both agree that any issues raised but not resolved during the weekend will result in a problem-solving program even if that means seeking more marriage counseling. So, if the only reason you'd go to a marriage encounter is to have fun together, get out your hiking boots and spend the day in the mountains instead."

It Has to Be Easy or He Won't Do It

Once Jack realized that marriage counseling wasn't a blaming process, he was enthusiastic in seeking greater compatibility with Linda. I gave them two "games" to play to get their renewal off to a good start.

LITTLE THINGS MEAN A LOT. You each agree on an activity that particularly delights you. It might be something your partner does for you (a back rub) or an outing that is especially pleasing. This activity is the game's reward.

Then, on Sunday evening, agree to the following: between Monday morning and dinnertime Friday, you'll each do one small act of kindness for the other. The act should be a little thing that means a lot to the other. The smaller the act, the better. Examples of such acts are cleaning golf clubs, cleaning out the car's ashtray, organizing a drawer, cleaning out a hairbrush, and polishing shoes. At this point no money should be spent on the act.

The goal of the game is to see who can correctly identify the small act of kindness done by the other. You should each come to dinner on Friday evening with a piece of paper on which you have written exactly what you did for your partner during the week. In the first week, you each get two guesses; in subsequent weeks, only one.

Whoever correctly identifies the act gets the reward. If both of you are correct, you both get your individual rewards; if neither is right, then there are no rewards that week. Take two days off from the game before starting again.

After the first two or three weeks, make the game more interesting by agreeing that a maximum of ten dollars can be spent in doing the small act of kindness (filling up the car's gas tank, buying a small handkerchief).

The main strategy of the game is to camouflage your act of kindness so that it's difficult to notice. Not only must you figure out what your partner likes, but you must also complete the kindness in a surreptitious manner.

128

The game will resensitize you to the little kindnesses that constitute a friendship. If your once-loving relationship has fallen into a negative rut, then chances are you've lost sight of the little things you used to do for each other. You should enjoy the rebirth the game will bring. Likewise, the very idea that you are spending time thinking and doing for your partner will improve the "stagnant" nature of your love.

The biggest problem in the Little-Things-Mean-a-Lot game is when one person forgets to play. This can be very painful for the other person. If your man has a history of procrastination, you should use small reminders during the first week of the game. You can do this by giving a hint once a day, reflecting upon a little thing that means a lot to you, or by putting up a sign in the kitchen that reads, "Little things mean a lot." Though no verbal hints are allowed after the first week, I suggest you leave the sign up throughout the game.

You can play the game as long as you wish, and you'll probably invent new dimensions to keep it exciting (for example, doing two things a week and doubling the reward). One of the side benefits of the game is that it can lead to a more stimulating discussion of other ways of renewing your love.

OPPOSITES ATTRACT. This exercise combines empathy and role-playing with a gaming spirit to teach you to accept each other's differences while acting in a more conciliatory fashion.

The main object of the exercise is for both partners to simultaneously and systematically reverse their respective patterns of behavior in a specific situation.

Begin by practicing the Opposites Attract exercise under loving circumstances. Select a conflicting trait that doesn't have a critical impact on the success of your relationship—for example, talkative versus quiet. With a noncompetitive spirit, act out a recent situation in which your partner talked incessantly and you were meek and unresponsive. Do it just long enough for both of you to re-create the scene. *Then, behave in an opposite manner.* Using your own words, talk incessantly while your partner nods his head, meekly says, "Mmm-hmm," and generally behaves in an unresponsive manner. Keep this general guideline in mind: once you and your partner have identified your respective patterns of behavior, select an opposite pattern and enact it simultaneously.

If you practice the Opposites Attract exercise several times in this manner, you'll have greater success applying it to a strenuous situation. For example, the next time you have a fight, call time out as soon as possible and go to separate rooms. Within five minutes, come together and conduct the Opposites Attract exercise. If you were typically defensive, you should become self-critical, while your partner, who is usually stubborn, proposes compromises.

It's essential that both partners in a relationship engage in the Opposites Attract exercise simultaneously. Otherwise, it's sure to fail and could possibly cause even more bad feelings. Failure is also assured if one or both partners adapt a competitive attitude toward the exercise (e.g., "My opposite was better than your opposite").

When Parents Interfere with the Relationship

"I've been married for two years," thirty-three-year-old Sandy said uncomfortably, "and I'm having trouble with parents getting in the way of my relationship with Sam.

"Sam's mother is widowed and a very sad case. She's the demanding type who'll call at any time of the day or night and expect him to come over immediately. He gets angry at her and admits that he doesn't know what to do. But he hates it when I suggest that he make her wait. He says I don't understand his predicament, because my parents are still healthy and don't need me like Sam's mother needs him. But he doesn't understand *my* situation with my mother—I'll get into that later."

Getting in the Middle

"Why can't you just ignore the situation?" I asked Sandy.

"Because Sam is often forced to choose between me and his mother. And she always wins. I can't tell you how often she's ruined an outing that I had planned for us."

"So what do you do?"

"Well, *if* she'll talk to me when she calls—she often won't—I tell her that Sam will come over later and do whatever it is she wants done. But that's not good enough. Sam has to call her as soon as he gets home and then he *has* to go right over. I don't like being in the middle like that."

"Why?"

"Why?" Sandy said with disbelief. "You think I *should* be in the middle?"

"Why not? You might be able to take some of the pressure off Sam and give yourself a little more freedom at the same time."

"But that won't solve the problem; that won't help Sam learn to cope with his mother."

"You're right," I answered, "and he probably won't ever learn to cope with her. And that's okay. How many of us really completely resolve the gap between ourselves and our parents? Not too many, I venture to say. We all have problems that are never solved."

"If I hear you correctly," Sandy said, "you want me to solve Sam's problem for him."

"No," I replied adamantly, "solve your problem, not his. Your problem is that you don't want Sam's mother getting to Sam and interrupting your plans. So, get in the middle and try to divert some of her demands."

"That's being very self-centered."

"Right you are. But don't confuse self-centered with selfish. Self-centered means promoting your own goals *within a moral guideline;* selfish means promoting your own goals *with no morality.*"

"So, what would I do if I were to solve my problem with Sam's mother in a self-centered manner?"

"Simply go over to her house when she calls and show her how good a problem-solver you can be. Then call the senior citizen's hotline and ask a volunteer to call your mother-in-law and get her involved in reading to the blind or a similar activity. When you tell Sam that his mother called, tell him that you want to take care of it; get his advice on what to tell her about her problem."

"And this will teach her to quit calling Sam?"

"I doubt it," I replied. "But it will teach her that you care about her, and that sometimes she'll have to rely upon you to run her errands. The bottom line of all this, of course, is that you reduce the number of times she interferes with your plans."

Sandy slowly began to implement the getting-in-the-middle program and realized that it gave her more control over the thing that was most upsetting her. There are, of course, negative side effects to this program. For example, it does not solve the problem, and it can actually increase an older parent's demands. However, if your man sees how you're trying to help, he may begin to work at the root of his problem.

Fogging

It was her success with her mother-in-law that inspired Sandy to confront her own mother. "Another major bone of contention between Sam and me is the way my mother meddles in our marriage. I've tried to point out the similarities between my mother and his, but he refuses to see them. I must admit that my mother can be more of a pill than his. At least his mother doesn't call other relatives and tell them our business."

"What have you tried to do?" I asked.

"Well," she said with a sigh, "I've tried to tell Mom how I feel, but she just gets weepy and then I feel guilty. I've also tried not answering her when she probes into my business, but she gets offended and then I feel guilty again. So, you see, I haven't had much luck."

In addition to helping her overcome her guilt, I told Sandy about *fogging*, a simple technique that is often effective in dealing with meddlesome people who get in the way of a couple's compatibility.

Fogging is a verbal response to another's probing question during which you talk but you don't communicate. The goal of fogging is to build a thick, confusing cloud of verbalizations between yourself and the person whom you want to fog. It's to be used with people who have no business prying into your private life or people you don't trust with personal information. Fogging permits you to respond in a friendly manner to an obtrusive question or comment without becoming defensive.

The key to successful fogging is being able to use another person's word or phrase as a tangent at which to divert the conversation. These "fogs" will give you the general idea:

- If a meddlesome parent says, "What will you say to your friends about Sam losing his promotion?" you could answer, "Oh, our friends are the greatest. Just the other day they suggested we go camping this summer."
- If a nosy acquaintance says, "Your best friend from high school just joined the country club you've been trying to get into," you might reply, "Wow, that reminds me, my high school reunion is next year. Did you ever go to a high school reunion?"
- If a gossipy neighbor says, "Was that your daughter in that car at two this morning?" you could answer, "You know, I'm having trouble sleeping, too."

In the first example, the fogger used the word *friends* to create the tangent. In the second example, the fogger paired the idea of high school with a reunion. The third fog was a bit more complicated in that the fogger used logic to arrive at a gentle confrontation.

If nosy people are good listeners, they'll hear your fog and recognize it for what it is—a tactful avoidance of the issue. However, since they're nosy, they may repeat their question. If they confront you about avoiding the question, they are showing themselves to be rude as well as nosy, which makes it infinitely easier for you to say, "You're right, I did avoid your question. I thought it was nicer than saying that it's none of your business."

"There's another benefit to be gained from fogging," I told Sandy. "Ask Sam to help you practice the fog. It might help him cope with his mother more effectively."

When He Forgets Your Birthday or Anniversary

Sandy quickly understood fogging and was eager to try it out. She used the rest of our session to ask me about what she said was a "small problem."

"I know Sam loves me," she said tentatively, "and he's not cheap when it comes to spending money on me. But he often forgets my birthday or our anniversary. I don't want to complain, but I feel hurt."

If you share Sandy's complaint, I recommend the following course of action:

First, understand the difference between a gift's commodity value and its intentional value. The commodity value measures the price of a gift; the intentional value reflects the thought that went into buying a gift. Men tend to be best acquainted with the former, women with the latter.

Second, accept the fact that you have little chance of directly increasing your man's understanding of intentional value. Be extremely careful to control any bitterness—"It's not fair that he's that way"—by saying aloud, "I love most things about him; his appreciation of gift-giving is not one of them."

Third, use *modeling* to try to teach him the importance of a gift's intentional value.

- A week before your birthday, make an appointment to go shopping together for your present. Tell him you need his help in buying a new sweater. Try on three sweaters, buy the one he likes best, and then go have lunch together.
- A day or two after buying him a present, explain your intentions behind getting him that particular present ("The color goes with your eyes," or, "You look great in blue"). Do not make reference to his forgetfulness.
- If he's unable to shop with you, buy yourself a special gift and, while showing it to him, say, "This is what you bought me for my birthday."

Finally, I suggest that you give serious thought to whether, for you, it's really "the thought that counts." You may be confusing your desire for your man to remember a special day with your need to be surprised. Admittedly, being surprised can be an exciting human experience. However, if you have a man who is kind and generous, but demonstrates his good intentions in a "nonsurprising" manner, maybe you should count your blessings and forgo your need to be surprised. It'll make you happier.

12.

HANDLING
HIS INSENSITIVITY

Grunts, snorts, and other bursts of air are expelled through his nose, though *I* is the only word that comes easily from his mouth. He talks violent sports or crude sexism while glancing about the room in search of admiration. When someone else tries to change the subject, he brings the topic of conversation back to himself. You should have little trouble recognizing this species as the *macho man*.

There's probably a piece of macho in every man. Perhaps it's a remnant of the caveman drive that made our prehistoric grandfathers cocky enough to think they could outsmart the wild boar. It's a disturbing behavior pattern, causing sensitive men and women alike to cringe in anger and frustration.

Confronting the Macho Man

Amy's encounter with her macho man was beginning to cause considerable strain in her marriage. "Randy and I have a group of friends that get together just about every weekend," she explained. "We usually order out for pizza or sandwiches and just sit around and talk or play a game. I look forward to the get-together as a kind of weekly therapy. We usually have a great time.

"That is, unless this one guy shows up. His name is Jimmy, and I can't stand him. He doesn't even have his coat off before he's saying something derogatory about women, or boasting about how some jock nearly killed another jock.

"What upsets me most," Amy continued, "is the way Randy acts when he gets around Jimmy. He tries to talk louder, brag more, and compete with Jimmy for the macho award, which he'll never win. He makes fun of women at work, and talks about our sex life in crude terms. What really digs the deepest is that Randy is not *really* that way."

"And what happens when you tell him about it?" I asked.

"Randy says I won't let him have fun. He says I'm too thin-skinned and that he likes to have fun on the weekends just as much as I do."

"And then what happens?" I asked.

"Not much, because I feel like such a bitch. I tell him how angry I get, but he thinks I'm being silly. When we're sitting there with our friends and he starts his macho impression, I give him dirty looks, or try to distract the group, or even make fun of what the guys are talking about. But it doesn't do me any good. I don't know what else to do."

Confronting the macho man requires skill, timing, and self-control, with an emphasis on the latter. If you can find a way to completely ignore macho behavior (if it happens infrequently, or if you really don't care about the man), I advise you to do so. If you can't, remember this general rule: any direct confrontation during the episode will most likely result in an *increase* in macho behavior.

It also helps to understand that macho behavior is a man's way of coping with his insecurity—an insecurity that comes from worrying about being rejected by "the guys," or being seen as "not man enough" by a woman. That's why most macho talk centers on physical aggression or sexual conquests.

Projected Imagery

Projected imagery is an indispensable tool in confronting the macho man. Here's how to make it work for you:

- Sharpen your imagination by practicing one or two of the imagery exercises suggested on page 67.
- Visualize your man as a little boy dressed up like John Wayne, but with a gun in one hand, a tattered blanket in the other, and a pacifier sticking out of his pocket. Project this image several times a day until you can close your eyes and see it clearly.
- Control your mothering response so that you don't feel sorry for your macho man–little boy.
- Keep the image ready for use during the actual encounter with macho man.

The therapeutic use of projected imagery is limitless. You can use it to overcome shyness, reduce your fear of rejection, improve your golf stroke, and increase your self-esteem and self-acceptance. To use it to accomplish a task, project an image of yourself completing each step of the task with efficiency and resolute determination. If you wish to study imagery in depth, see the appendix for further reading.

Once you've mastered projected imagery, follow these steps in confronting your man's macho behavior next time others bring it out in him.

Avoid pushing his "macho button." That is, do not yell, scream, or belittle him; do not laugh at his silliness or criticize him; and do not judge his behavior with such remarks as, "Quit being childish, Randy." Rather, remove yourself from the room in the most unobtrusive manner possible, for example, by excusing yourself to go to the bathroom.

In private, close your eyes and project the image you've been practicing. To avoid feeling sorry for him, say aloud, "He may be an insecure little boy right now, but I want a man, not a boy."

Once your anger has dissipated, return to the room, and, without saying a word, *go over to your man and stand beside him*. This nonverbal message *may* give him the support he needs to extricate himself from his whirlwind of macho talk. Do not reach out to touch him. If he touches you in such a way as to call attention to himself or uses you to demonstrate his macho behavior, move away from him immediately and, if possible, again leave the

137

room. If circumstances prohibit another exit, move as far away from him as possible and talk to someone else. *Do not say anything to him.*

Talk to him the next day about your concerns and use denominalization (see page 106) to make a specific request; for example, "When I come over and stand beside you, would you please ask me how I'm doing or if I'm having a good time?" The purpose of this question is for your man to forget about himself for a moment and consider your feelings.

If this program doesn't work, you may wish simply to avoid parties where there's a lot of macho talk. The most confrontational action would be to prearrange an alternative ride home and leave the party after the loving confrontation failed. You should warn your man of this possibility.

"There's an outside chance," I told Amy, "that a more direct confrontation might work. It would occur a minute or two after you'd been standing beside Randy. You would say, 'Come in the kitchen with me, would you please?' If he asks why, just tell him you have something very private to say to him. When you get to the kitchen, give him a big hug and tell him you love him. Do not mention the macho talk."

"How would that help?" Amy asked.

"You would be breaking up the synergistic force that had trapped Randy."

"The what?"

"Imagine that macho talk is a cyclone and that Randy gets trapped in the center. Your action breaks him out of the whirlwind and gives him the opportunity to move away from the group."

"And what if he goes right back into it?"

"There's nothing you can do about that," I said. "However, the next day, tell Randy how good it felt to be in the kitchen with him. And then tell him how bad it feels when the macho whirlwind takes him away from you."

When He Doesn't Think of Your Feelings

Faye is a cheerful woman whose complaint may rank at the top of any woman's list. "Stan doesn't take the time to think about my needs," she said. "I feel as if I could be lying in the street and he'd say, 'What's for supper, hon?' And you know what's worse, Dr. Dan? I love him like nobody's business."

"It's not all bad, then, is it?" I asked.

"Not at all. We have a great time together, except when it comes to him helping me. For example, his mother was over last Sunday, and he knows what a royal pain she can be. Well, she started lecturing me about Adam, our ten-year-old, saying how I should put him in a gifted class at school, how I should spend more time with him since he's obviously a genius.

"Now I'll grant you that Adam is smart, but he's not a genius. Well, anyway, I looked over at Stan and rolled my eyes to the ceiling in desperation. He got up and left the table! When I asked him later about leaving me without saying something, he shrugged it off and said, 'You were doing fine, babe, you didn't need me.' I've told him a hundred times that I need his understanding and help, especially with his mother."

Stan lacked empathy, an attribute that every professional agrees is essential for a successful relationship, yet is difficult to define. Bringing cheer into someone's life, being able to walk a mile in another's footsteps, and the giving of one's time and attention to someone else are all examples of empathy in action. For our purposes, empathy will be defined as the ability to share one's time with another.

Though not exact in its findings, research on empathy concludes that empathetic people are less anxious, more self-directed, able to read social situations, and more motivated to work with people. People who are low in empathy tend to be nervous, selfish, and given to stress-related problems.

I gave Faye the following behavioral descriptions to analyze Stan's empathy as well as her own. See how you and your man come out.

Does he/do you . . .

> . . . read and respond to a variety of signals coming from another (such as sexual, intimate, hurting, joyful, sad)?
> . . . seem to be aware of the impression he makes/you make on other people?

... have the ability to predict with some accuracy how
you/he will respond emotionally to certain situations?

... have insight into his/your own motives and behavior?

... take your/his motives into account when interpreting
your/his behavior?

If you answered yes to one of these questions, you probably
answered yes to almost all of them. Four or five yes answers
indicates a strong sense of empathy.

Double-check your evaluation by seeing whether these behavioral descriptions apply to you or your man.

Does he/do you . . .

... not vary his/your behavior when faced with different
interpersonal cues?

... judge others in conventional terms like "proper" and
"it's the correct thing to do"?

... become quite bothered by uncertainty?

... make a habit of blaming others?

... handle anxiety by ignoring the problem?

If you answered yes to most of the questions in the first survey,
you should have answered no to most of the questions in the
second. Faye concluded that Stan's empathy was weak, especially
his ability to predict how someone else would react to a situation.

As I told Faye, "These surveys should help you realize that
Stan isn't ignoring you because he doesn't care about you, but
because he doesn't know what to do."

"Oh, I know he cares," Faye said, "but this just helps me
understand why he seems to have a brick for a brain."

Faye's warm smile told me that she cared deeply for Stan
and that with a bit of cooperation on his part, she might be
able to teach him to improve his empathy skills.

Empathy Exercise

"I suggest you use the *empathy exercise* to try and help Stan improve
his overall sensitivity toward you. This exercise is actually a seri-

ous 'game' involving guessing how another person feels in a given situation."

"Okay," Faye said in her typical upbeat fashion, "tell me what to do."

"I want you to practice the empathy exercise at least three times a week for the next few weeks."

The empathy exercise has two goals: to help you better understand your man's reaction to key situations in his life (for example, his mother's meddling) and to slowly help him improve his ability to understand your feelings.

If you use this exercise to sensitize your man to your feelings, I suggest you approach him at a comfortable moment and say, "I want to quiz myself on something and I need your help." After assuring him that it will be fun for both of you, either ask him to describe an interesting situation he encountered that day, or recall a situation from the recent past, and ask for his help in describing it accurately.

Then say, "I want to see how close I can come to describing your internal reaction to that situation." When you describe his internal reaction, use a procedure I call *emotional analogies*. That means you say, "I bet you felt like _____." Use your own background and interests in creating the appropriate analogy. If you're interested in horses, you might say, "I bet you felt like a horse that had been ridden hard and given nothing to drink." Or, if home economics is your forte, you might say, "I bet you felt like a bowl of jelly left out in the sun."

If you have trouble finding an appropriate analogy, you can always refer to a child's world. "I bet you felt like a child who got sand kicked in his face."

Then ask your man how close you were to the truth and encourage him to use an emotional analogy to clarify the truth. Repeat this process two or three times.

I was careful to remind Faye not to push the game if Stan didn't want to play and to be sure she used the words *internal reaction* instead of *feeling*.

"Why can't I say *feeling?*" she asked.

I explained, "I'm sure you're aware of the thousands of women who are forever complaining that men don't express their feelings.

141

One of the reasons for this is that many men have a feeling-identification deficit. They simply have a difficult time attaching a common emotional label to an internal arousal state. You'll have much greater luck sharing Stan's feelings and teaching him to be sensitive to your feelings if you use a more analytical concept—*internal reaction*. His male brain will be more in tune with the logical, rational quality of that concept. And it will be much easier for him to express what he is, in fact, feeling.

"That's rather sneaky, isn't it?" Faye said, obviously enjoying the idea of the game. "It's kind of like teaching me to brainwash him."

"To brainwash him," I said, "you'd have to be able to control his mind. And we already know you don't have that power."

"Boy, do we know that!"

"The empathy exercise should not be an arduous or painful process," I said. "If it starts to head in that direction, stop it and move on to something else."

If Stan wanted to play the game, I suggested that Faye start with an easy situation; for example, what her internal reaction is when his mother lectures her about Adam. "If he fails," I explained, "clarify your reaction using your own emotional analogy and ask him if he'd like to try again."

"He's so competitive," Faye said, "that he'll want to beat my score."

"That's why you don't keep score," I replied. "You don't want competitiveness entering into an exercise for empathy."

I explained to Faye that empathy has many long-lasting benefits, one of which is physical. "Empathy prolongs life in two ways. It opens up a whole new world for a man like Stan to explore—the world experienced by you—and it takes his mind off himself, helping him to relax and take life as it comes."

"And," Faye said with a sparkle in her eyes, "it'll make him much more thoughtful toward his wife. Both of us know what *that* means."

He Takes Me for Granted

"Keith is the neighborhood angel, but he's a devil at home," Gayle said, her frustration mounting. "He'll run over to the neighbors to help them with a problem, but when it comes to something I need help with, he 'forgets.' It wouldn't be so bad if he didn't take me for granted."

"What do you mean by 'taking you for granted'?" I asked.

"Keith is an avid tennis player. When he comes home from a game, he throws his dirty athletic clothes on the floor of the laundry room. He expects me to wash and fold them and have them lying by the door the next day. I've been doing it for years, but I'm getting sick and tired of it."

"Have you considered the alternatives?" I asked.

"Yes," Gayle said, obviously distressed. "Either I wash the clothes and receive no thanks, or I don't wash them and listen to him complain."

"Would you agree," I said, "that by acting as Keith's slave, you invite his disrespect?"

"Yes."

"Would you also agree that the two alternatives you've considered—to wash or not to wash—are inadequate?"

"Absolutely."

"Then how about a third alternative—a compromise of the two?"

"I'd love it," Gayle said.

Strategic Withdrawal

I instructed Gayle on the application of *strategic withdrawal* to her problem with Keith's dirty clothes. Gayle would withdraw her laundrying behavior in small progressive stages, giving Keith clear indication that she was changing her "slavish" behavior.

First she would specify her complaint using denominalization (see page 106). She would say, "Keith, I would appreciate your not throwing your dirty athletic clothes on the floor and expecting me to wash them without ever asking me to and without ever saying thanks."

"I've said that a thousand times," Gayle interrupted.

"But I'll bet each time you said it, there was disapproval in your voice, just like a mother," I countered.

"Well . . ." Gayle hesitated. "I think you're probably right."

"If so, you can bet that he's learned not to hear you. You

need to state your complaint in the most rational, precise manner possible. Then tell Keith exactly what you plan to do, and do it." I suggested that she say, "If you want your dirty clothes cleaned on a day other than laundry day, put them in the washer and start it and I'll put them in the dryer." Gayle would have better luck if she slowly eliminated her slave role, instead of simply stopping it cold turkey.

The four stages of Gayle's strategic withdrawal from picking up her man's athletic clothes were as follows:

FIRST DAY. Point out his clothes lying about and say, "Three days from now, I won't pick them up." Then pick them up and wash them as before. Do not demand that he pick them up, since this sounds too much like a mother.

SECOND DAY. Repeat the statement and indicate that only two days remain. But instead of folding the clothes and putting them by the door, put them unfolded in a sack on top of the dryer.

THIRD DAY. Say, "This is the last day I'll pick up any of your athletic clothes and wash them. Please put them in the washer when you get home." On this day, leave the clothes in the dryer or sitting on the floor.

FOURTH DAY. Do not touch Keith's clothes unless they are in the washer. If tempted to do it just one more time, Gayle should say aloud to herself, "I'll never get any consideration if I don't act as if I deserve it."

Once you've identified a situation in which your man takes you for granted, divide the situation into three or four stages you could use to slowly withdraw your support or help. If you're not sure how fast to withdraw from the situation, it's best to err on the side of moving too slowly. Don't worry if you get confused or can't complete the program. The fact that you tried something different and explained it clearly will likely have an impact on your man.

The main justification for strategic withdrawal is that by not acting in an excessive manner, a woman helps her man get the idea that he can't take her for granted. Both partners have a bad habit to break, and it's better for their relationship to do that in stages, hence the concept of *strategic*.

When His Feelings Turn to Stone

Gayle returned to my office six or seven months later. She had had such great success with the strategic withdrawal program that she now wanted to work on another, more complicated problem. "I'm here," she said with a strong sense of self-esteem, "to make my marriage even better. I want to share more of Keith's life."

Gayle knew that I worked in specifics. "What do you mean?" I asked.

"I've always known that Keith is a private person, and I've tried to accept the way he keeps me at arm's length. But I don't like living with a man who can turn to stone just when he's beginning to feel something. I don't want Keith to shut me out anymore."

"You're changing the rules a bit, aren't you?" I said.

"What do you mean?"

"You've known from the day you married Keith how he handles his emotions. And you've even said that you've learned to live with it. But now you're asking him to change his stripes—to learn a whole new way of relating to you."

"Is that wrong?"

"No," I answered. "But what you're asking could take forever and then some."

But Gayle was oozing confidence. "Hey, my relationship isn't that bad. Keith doesn't have to turn into a mushy person—I wouldn't like him if he did. I'll be happy with him no matter what happens. I just want a little bit of the sensitivity that's inside him. And you yourself said that men would be happier and live longer if they learned to share their vulnerabilities."

When I asked Gayle to describe how Keith shuts her out, she told me about a recent situation in the neighborhood. A child had been lost and Keith had organized a search party. He led searchers day and night for two days. When the police finally found the child, Keith was physically and emotionally exhausted.

"When I asked him how he felt," Gayle explained, "he turned red and stood there. I could see his feelings all over his face. He had been deeply touched. Yet he snapped at me and told me that it was no big deal and that he just needed to get some sleep. He loves our dog Sparky, but he even tried to hit him when Sparky didn't get out of the way fast enough. I could tell he wanted to talk about it, but instead he turned to stone."

The biggest risk for any woman who faces a like situation is falling into the trap of playing "junior shrink"—that is, trying to analyze what's going on inside her man. It's very tempting to think that if only you can understand why he turns cold, you'll discover a crack in his "defenses" and help him express himself.

Emotional Shaping

Instead of getting caught up in the fruitless pursuit of the whys and wherefores of his coldness, you're better off implementing a slow program of *emotional shaping*. It combines elements already described—the empathy exercise, strategic withdrawal, and projected imagery—with patience and an understanding that progress will only come in small steps.

The focal point of emotional shaping is the projection of the "good angel–bad angel" image. Picture an angel sitting on each of your man's shoulders. The good angel wants him to open up and share his feelings with you; the bad angel wants him to turn to stone. Because of his cultural background and training, the bad angel may be stronger than the good one.

The best way for you to confront the bad angel is to do whatever you can to strengthen the good angel ("shaping" positive feelings). Follow these steps when confronting the coldness of the bad angel:

- Gradually withdraw from his coldness by remaining quiet, leaving the room, or leaving the house if you must. Ignore any outbursts of temper.
- Wait until he calms down or his coldness subsides, and then

ask him what his "internal reaction" was during his period of being upset.

- Explain how you reacted to his emotional moment by using an analogy. For example, "I felt like I was in the eye of a hurricane."
- If he still shuts you out, *do not push him to talk*.
- Do not fight with his bad angel. Any struggle with the bad angel will only make it stronger. You want to *extinguish* the bad angel's influence, not draw attention to it.

"When Keith shuts you out," I explained to Gayle, "the bad angel is in control. *Leave him alone.* I know it sounds a little awkward, but the strength of your confrontation is to wait until the bad angel backs off and then see if you can use one of my techniques to get the good angel to talk.

"If Keith can sense that the good angel is slowly gaining strength, and if he really understands the benefit of emotional openness and wants it for himself, then he will gradually begin to battle the bad angel. That's why I told you that this emotional shaping program requires time, patience, and your acceptance of a less-than-perfect goal."

"I don't expect perfection anymore," Gayle said sincerely. "I understand that Keith will move at his own pace—he's that kind of guy and I love him for it. Now that I know what to do, I'll ignore the bad angel and do everything I can to support the good one. And whatever I get, I'll be happy. It's more than I've got now."

13.

STOPPING
HIS MENTAL ABUSE

Mental abuse is a tricky situation that is difficult for even the most trained professional to evaluate. On the one hand, there is militant indifference to your needs and stark disregard for your integrity. On the other, you are the one who sits there and takes it, often coming back for more. You say that you love him, yet love should give you strength, not force you into the depths of a painful and cyclical trap.

If you feel that your man is guilty of mental abuse, you owe it to yourself and your relationship to try and stop it. I don't think that means you must automatically leave him. There are other steps you can take short of leaving that might help him wake up and see what he's doing.

This chapter covers three major areas of mental abuse—mistrust, loneliness, and a general disregard for integrity.

When You Don't Trust Him

"Lee and I have had two rocky years," Shana began. "About six months before he turned forty, he had an affair. Well, he said he never slept with her, but it still hurt. Lee is such a sweet and gullible guy, I'm sure he just stumbled into it. He said that he was sorry and wanted to stay married.

"However, it wasn't two months later that he stumbled into another mistake. He told my neighbor about my getting raped when I was in college. He said that he thought she already knew, but he should've known better. I've only shared that with him and my best friend.

"Things have been going pretty well the past few months, except that the past keeps gnawing at me. I know I should trust Lee, but I think I'm afraid to."

Trust Renewal Program

Shana and Lee had to embark on the *trust renewal program*. If you are having a trust problem with your man, encourage him to join you in studying and applying the guidelines that fit your situation. This is one program that cannot be successful unless your man participates with you. As always, do not browbeat him; simply take him through the steps, assuming that he, too, wants to improve your mutual trust.

1. ORIENTATION. The level of trust between two people is often measured by the willingness of each to disclose personal information. Recent research suggests that self-disclosure in areas such as family background, emotions, religion, and relationships with other people is closely connected to intimacy and commitment. If your trust has been lowered, then it follows that you don't wish to disclose personal information to your partner; if that persists, you can expect your intimacy and commitment to suffer.

2. THE TRUST QUIZ. Take the following trust quiz. Indicate on a scale from 1 to 10 (10 being the highest) how strongly you agree with each of the following statements:

- My partner is primarily interested in his or her own welfare.
- There are times when my partner cannot be trusted.
- My partner is dishonest with me.
- My partner rarely shares personal and confidential information with me.

- My partner is not sincere in his promises.
- My partner does not show me enough consideration.
- My partner does not treat me fairly and justly.
- I can't count on my partner.

Get your average score by totaling your numbers and dividing by 8. If your average exceeds 7, your trust is very poor and you can expect your love to erode unless you take remedial action. If your average is between 4 and 6, improving your self-disclosure should result in increased trust. If your average is 3 or under, it's likely you don't have a trust problem in your relationship.

Trust is another of those areas of a relationship in which it's nearly impossible to determine the extent of one's responsibility. All you can do is to improve your part of the trust formula and hope your partner reciprocates.

3. DESENSITIZATION. Improving trust means gradually overcoming the fear of betrayal. The *desensitization* program will permit you to rebuild trust in small steps. It is a process whereby you gradually reduce your fear of some object or situation. In this case, the situation you will learn not to fear is having your man betray your trust. Desensitization to the fear of betrayal can only be successful if you (a) give your man the opportunity to keep your trust and (b) he proves himself worthy of that trust.

Construct a hierarchy of personal information, ranging from something you wouldn't mind telling a stranger ("I don't like people who lie") to something of a highly sensitive nature (being raped). An example of a hierarchy might include, in ascending order of sensitivity: I flunked math in high school; I have a bad temper; I was a virgin when I got married; my mother was an alcoholic; I don't believe in God; I was raped when I was fifteen.

Be prepared to share the details of each step in the hierarchy. If your man already knows one bit of information, try to share it in such a way that you disclose a new dimension to the story.

Before beginning this desensitization program, explain to your man that you're trying to learn to trust him again. Tell him that the latest studies indicate that a good relationship is built on weakness. This seemingly contradictory finding means that when two people know each other's weaknesses, they protect one another.

The desensitization program will take time. You should wait a few days between sharing items on the low end of the hierarchy and up to a few weeks between sharing items on the high end. The greater the sensitivity of the sharing, the more you need to trust him. You'll only be assured of that trust if your man treats the information confidentially.

Thus, if you admit to having a bad temper, and your man lets it slip during a social gathering, brings it up during an argument, or otherwise betrays your trust, you'll have clear evidence that you should withhold any further self-disclosure until you can resolve the underlying lack of respect he has for your secrets. However, if the secret is kept, you can feel more confident in sharing the next item on the trust hierarchy. In this manner, you slowly build or rebuild trust, and with it, intimacy and commitment.

The desensitization program will not be completely successful unless your man eventually begins to participate with you. While you shouldn't coerce him into sharing his own hierarchy of personal information, your example should be reason enough for him to follow your lead. If he doesn't, I suggest you discontinue this part of the program and consider the possibility that your man doesn't want to work at your relationship.

4. ELIMINATING THE CAUSE. If an extramarital sexual affair is or has been a threat to your relationship, you'll want to pay careful attention to this step in the trust renewal program. Familiarize yourself with the material in this section even if extramarital sex is not an immediate threat to you. Share the following information with your man in whatever way you think is best for you.

A recent research paper cited four major causes of marital infidelity: a person's genetic and psychological need for a new sex partner; the availability of such a partner; the nature of the sexual relationship with the primary partner; and the person's fantasies about having a new sex partner.

Need. Women tend to have less physical need for new partners, so they should examine their psychological needs. They may want more nonsexual physical contact from their man. If a man says he needs more physical sex, he should consider the possibility that this need is, in fact, a camouflage for his need for more psychological contact.

Availability. Since we live in a highly mobile society, practically anyone could find an extramarital sex partner if he or she wanted to. If an extramarital affair is or has been a concern for you, you're well advised to identify times and places when you might meet a potential sex partner. You needn't avoid those places, just be aware of the temptation that resides there.

Satisfaction. Be honest in reviewing your satisfaction with your sex life. Are there things you want that you're not getting? Likewise, be honest with yourself in evaluating the other extreme— are you expecting too much from your sex life? Many couples find it very difficult to find the happy medium that lies between boring, repetitive sex and the thrill and excitement of "honeymoon sex."

Fantasies. Finally, take an inventory of the quality and quantity of your fantasies about having sex with other people. If these fantasies are specific and involve real people who are available to you as possible sex partners, you've increased your chances of becoming involved with one of them.

If a sexual affair has hurt the trust between you and your partner, be sure to conduct this analysis within the guilt-free atmosphere of self-acceptance. The one who had the affair should say aloud, "I'm not a terrible person for wanting to have/having an affair. I simply need to know why I want it/did it and then make a decision based upon that information."

Once you've identified the causes of the sexual affair, or of wanting to have one, and assuming that you want to reestablish trust by moving back toward monogamy, you must begin to eliminate these causes.

I suggest that you focus on the second two of the four causes outlined above. Consult the sexual revitalization program in Chapter 9, Dealing with Sexual Problems.

Here's how the program worked in Shana and Lee's case.

Facing his middle age, Lee had what many call a midlife crisis, although it was premature and short-lived. He had been fantasizing for several months about having sex with a younger woman at work. Meanwhile, sex with Shana had deteriorated and was made even worse by a temporary bout with impotence.

On several occasions, Lee had drinks with this other woman after work, and then they necked and petted in the parking lot. His terrible guilt prohibited him from actually having sex with the woman. Although he didn't realize it at the time, Lee was caught up in a "burst of freedom," an exciting flashback to his late teen years.

Lee had three goals to achieve, all of which involved Shana. First, he had to explain his sexual needs to his wife so that she could learn how to better meet them. Second, he had to accept his occasional impotence as normal and quit making it worse than it was. Third, he had to control his sexual fantasies. Essentially, that meant that while his fantasy life would continue, he should control it so that he didn't fantasize about having sex with a specific woman; nor should he permit sexual fantasies to replace asking Shana for more satisfying sex.

5. FORGIVENESS. Shana was creating misery for herself by trying to forget Lee's mistakes. In trying to forget, she was unintentionally setting herself up to keep the past alive. If you're trying to forgive your man for a mistake, do not attempt to forget. In fact, the more you force yourself to forget, the more you'll remember, the more you'll hurt, and the less likely you'll be able to forgive.

Technically, forgetting will never occur. However, with each new and enriching love experience you share with your man, your memory will dull. Eventually the memory of the mistake will fade to the point that it will have little if any impact on your love life.

Forgiveness is not something that happens simply because you wish it. Forgiveness is the *end result* of your personal growth. The growth occurs when you listen to your man's reasons for his mistake and recognize that he's honestly working to eliminate the cause and regain your trust; when you determine how you can help meet his needs; and when you exercise compassion in seeing that he's not the strong, perfect man you may have believed him to be.

When you forgive, you take a load off yourself, open yourself

153

up to new possibilities of loving, and become stronger as an individual. If and when you relapse into suspiciousness, recall your man's attempts to show you his trustworthiness. This will chase the memory, and with it, your suspiciousness. If you realize that he's not working to improve trust between you, then you have the problem of ill will (consult Chapter 16).

Forgiving takes time, and you'll likely backslide into sarcasm or another form of anger from time to time. Have patience with yourself and apologize to your partner.

The trust renewal program can be used in situations other than sexual infidelity. If you feel abused because your man behaves in an untrustworthy manner, apply the same five steps, uncovering and eliminating the cause relating to your situation. This program is time-consuming, but it may be the most important one presented in this book.

When He Leaves You Lonely Too Often

"What it all comes down to, Dr. Kiley," Trish said, settling back into her chair, "is that I love Tom more than he loves me. I thought love was a cure for loneliness, but not in my case."

Trish had been very specific in answering my question, "What exactly do you want to see changed?" She offered many instances in which Tom's work and play prevented him from spending time with her. He was often out of town overnight on business; when he was in town, he had evening meetings; and he played basketball in the winter and baseball in the summer.

"And when he *is* with me," Trish continued, "I feel no warmth coming from him. It's as if he's not really there. I know it sounds strange, but that's how it feels."

I told Trish that at this point in her relationship, she had to assume that Tom *did* love her but was not aware of his abuse. She had no evidence to the contrary. "Are you sure he understands how you feel?" I asked.

"Maybe not," she replied. "I do know that I feel foolish for feeling lonely. It doesn't make any sense. I have a nice home, a good job, and despite what I say, Tom is very good to me. See how I contradict myself."

"If you are this ambivalent," I said, "then there's every reason to believe that Tom dismisses your complaints as something that will pass. You must first give yourself the right to feel lonely, and then, give Tom the right to be wrong. It seems to me that you are wrong for not accepting the lonely side of yourself, and Tom is wrong for not giving you more support."

Too often a woman believes she has communicated her complaint to her man in clear, unequivocal terms, when in fact her words were couched in ambivalence or uncertainty and her man simply didn't hear what she was trying to say.

Loneliness is not an easy thing to communicate. It stems from a complicated interplay of social, psychological, developmental, and economic factors. Your brand of loneliness may feel the same as the next person's, but it is likely to be unique to your personality. You can't expect your man to understand such a complex emotion unless you've made your feelings *very* clear.

If you feel lonely because you lack support from your man, you'll want to make certain that you communicate this feeling to him clearly and concisely. Below is an abbreviated but reliable version of a loneliness scale. Indicate how often you have the feeling described in each statement on a scale of 1 = never; 2 = rarely; 3 = sometimes; 4 = often.

I don't feel in tune with people around me.

No one really knows me well.

I can't find companionship when I want it.

People are around me but not with me.

If your total score is 15 or 16, your loneliness is moderate to severe and you may need help with it. If it's between 11 and 14, your loneliness is mild, and probably not too great a problem. If it's 10 or under, loneliness shouldn't be a problem at all.

For each statement to which you gave a score of 3 or 4, spend a few minutes and write out an example of when you felt that way. If it involves your man, write two or three paragraphs describing his actions *without judging him*. You will be able to write such a judgment-free minijournal if you see yourself as the proverbial "fly on the wall" observing the events.

Once you've completed your notes, you'll have an accurate description of your feeling. *Give your notes to your man*, saying, "I want to make sure you understand how I'm feeling. I get a little confused, so I thought it would be best to write it down. I'll talk about it if you want to."

When you talk to your man about your feelings, you'll want to concentrate on the three major causes of loneliness, all of which are related to each other.

- *Low self-esteem.* The automatic thought, "I'm a failure," is a major contributor to low self-esteem. If your loneliness is related to low self-esteem, chances are you believe you're a failure *in your man's eyes*. You need him to praise your efforts and accomplishments more often.
- *Worry about rejection.* Worrying about your man rejecting you in some way and anticipating the worst possible outcome of a social encounter can easily result in withdrawal from people in general and your man in particular. Ask your man to support you in taking a risk, and have him remind you that other people are just as worried about rejection as you are.
- *Depression.* Inactivity, withdrawal, and proliferation of negative thoughts can result in depression. If your loneliness is related to depression, make certain you explain this very carefully to your man (make a tape recording of your thoughts if writing seems like too big a task).

Trish's loneliness was closely related to worrying about Tom's rejection. Because of that, she felt as if she was bothering him whenever she tried to explain how she felt. As a result, she failed to make herself heard and understood. It was a cycle that had to be broken.

Trish found it very helpful to record her feelings on a small cassette recorder. Not only did Tom hear the loneliness in her voice, but she also felt better merely talking out her feelings. I reminded her to take care in protecting the privacy of the tapes.

What is more, Tom used the tape recorder to give Trish a blow-by-blow description of his activity while he was on the road. Trish played these recordings when Tom was away, and it helped her loneliness a great deal.

When You Have to Do All the Work

"Gene's afraid to accept responsibility," Marcie said, getting to the point immediately. "Either that, or he's just plain lazy. I'm not sure which it is. Maybe it's both."

Marcie was an attractive, vibrant twenty-seven-year-old woman who, despite her independent nature, was deeply involved with 25-year-old Gene, a man who had not yet grown up.

"Gene and I have lived together for fourteen months," she said. "He has trouble holding a job, so I get stuck with all the bills and have to give him spending money. If I don't give him money, he criticizes me for not supporting him while he's finding himself, and then he gets money from his parents."

"And you keep supporting him," I said.

"I know Gene loves me," Marcie said softly, "and we want to get married. But if he's constantly searching for his career, he won't have a reliable income. He says it will change soon. How long can I wait?"

Quid Pro Quo

I obviously couldn't give Marcie an answer to this question, but I did give her a new way of looking at her relationship with Gene, and with men in general. It's called the *quid pro quo*— the literal translation being "this for that." If your man disregards your integrity, I encourage you to apply this viewpoint to your situation.

The *quid pro quo* is an unspoken bargain that develops in every relationship and acts as a set of rules governing that relationship. It's the balance a relationship attains in the first few months and then seeks to sustain as long as the relationship lasts. If the balance is equitable, the relationship will endure; if it isn't, love

157

will suffer. The *quid pro quo* is not a conscious decision; instead, it's an exchange of accommodations built on individual personalities and supposedly based on the law of reciprocity.

"When you first started dating Gene," I said slowly, "you may have found his irresponsibility endearing because it meant he needed you. Your love caused you to overlook his laziness. Whenever you supported his irresponsibility, he concluded that you endorsed it. The roles—he's irresponsible, you are his protector—were established early on.

"The rules of your and Gene's relationship have to be changed. To do that he must be willing to alter his pattern of irresponsibility and you must be willing to alter your protectiveness."

"It sounds as if I'm responsible for Gene's laziness," she surmised.

"I know," I replied. "It's tough to be involved with another person and not feel responsible for him. But ask yourself this: are you so powerful that you could change Gene from a responsible man into a lazy jerk in fourteen months? I mean, you're good, but you're not *that* good!"

Marcie was laughing. "Then how did this happen?"

"You and your man fell into a routine, and unintentionally, you began to protect him from himself. I'm sure he has other, more loving traits, like . . ."

"You bet," she interrupted. "That's why I'm here. I know he is the right man for me, if I can just find the key to his sense of responsibility."

"Be careful," I warned. "That sounds as if you're going to play God and make him change. Remember—you can be a teacher, but you're still a human being."

"So," she said sadly, "there's nothing I can do?"

"On the contrary," I said with a smile, "there's almost no limit to the things you can do, *if* you first accept the boundaries of your power."

Virtues/Vices Continuum

In addition to the trust renewal program, I gave Marcie the *virtues/vices continuum* program. This program is designed to help you evaluate your attraction to your man, and then explore ways of helping him overcome his vices by reemphasizing his virtues. It's built upon the notion that people choose partners who possess qualities that have a bad as well as a good side to them. The chooser may find a trait virtuous at first, only later to discover that it has a dark side. Then it becomes a vice.

If you want to use the virtues/vices continuum program to teach your man to overcome his vices, begin by rating your man on a scale from 1 to 10 on the virtues and vices listed below. Give him a 10 if he's perfect in the virtue, and a 1 if he's perfect in the vice. If his particular virtues or vices are not included, add them, making sure you list the two extremes.

VIRTUE	VICE
Adventurous	Takes no chances
Sociable	Reclusive
Good-natured	Irritable
Conscientious	Irresponsible
Cooperative	Negative
Tidy	Careless
Mild, Gentle	Headstrong
Persevering	Fickle, Quitting
Calm	Excitable
Intellectual	Unreflective

Now, ask yourself the question: "What attracted me most to him at the beginning?" Select a virtue that answers the question, and then think of the opposite—the vice. Chances are the vice is one of the major problems you're having with your man.

Marcie decided that Gene's adventurousness was what first attracted her to him, and that now his reluctance to take a risk bothered her the most.

"This virtue/vice continuum," I explained, "becomes the focal point of your present difficulty with your man. Stick with this continuum when talking to Gene about what you want to see changed in him. Remind him of his adventurousness when you first knew him and encourage him to use it in deciding upon what career to pursue."

I then advised Marcie to repeat the evaluation, only this time on herself. "Obviously you should involve Gene in this program as soon as he's willing, but he can certainly help you decide on your virtue/vice continuum."

"It shouldn't be difficult to find your major virtue/vice," I said. "You probably already know Gene's biggest complaint about you."

"Oh, yes," Marcie replied. "He says that I act as if I'm always right. Yet he used to *like* the fact that I would stand up for myself."

"That's the point of the virtue/vice continuum. It's possible that your assertiveness has become abrasive. What was once seen as a virtue now appears to be a vice."

"So how can I use this to influence Gene?" Marcie asked.

"Evaluate yourself and see if you're happy with how you've grown in being assertive. Could you soften your approach a bit? Might you be overreacting in certain situations? Do you repeat yourself too often? Think about these things. Then decrease the vice and increase the virtue. You will be changing your part of the *quid pro quo*. If Gene is at all interested in improving your relationship, this soft confrontation will likely result in a decrease in his cautiousness and an increase in his adventurousness."

"I must have missed something." Marcie looked confused. "How will my working on my virtue cause Gene to work on his?"

"You can be sure he watches you like a hawk," I said with conviction. "You, like most women, don't realize how much of an influence you really have on your man."

"That's hard to believe," she said with a look of exasperation. "He seems to delight in ignoring me."

"Well, if you're going to try to stay with this man and make your relationship work," I said, "you're going to have to accept the fact that Gene's growth will be slow and will greatly depend upon the example you set."

"What do I do about the money problems while he's taking his time to grow?"

160

"You have to confront him as rationally as you possibly can. Use the *financial confrontation procedure* to say, 'I can't carry the total burden of paying our bills. If you want to study our budget and see where the money goes, great! But I can no longer be responsible for your spending money, car insurance, or health club dues. I'm sorry.' "

"He'd have a fit," Marcie blurted out. "And he'd accuse me of not caring."

"Simplify things for yourself, Marcie," I said supportively. "Decide if you're going to stand up for what you believe is right. Either that, or you continue to contribute to Gene's irresponsibility."

I suggested to Marcie that she separate the "must-pay" bills from the ones that could be carried over a few months. "The reality is," I emphasized, "that you are the responsible person in this relationship. And that isn't going to change in the immediate future. If you don't make rational decisions, your own security will be in jeopardy."

Marcie's budget should have included her own spending money and her savings. It should not have include secondary expenses for Gene, such as his spending money. I knew Marcie would feel defensive about the financial confrontation, so I reminded her not to lecture Gene as his mother might.

Like so many women in her shoes, Marcie had to face the daily temptation to be lured back into the same old habits. Behind this temptation was the question, "What can I do to make him change?" I had to remind her of this, so I told her to use overt self-instruction with a card on her mirror that read, "Remember, you're just a person, not God."

14.

BUILDING
YOUR SOCIAL LIFE

As children, we all knew how to play; it came naturally. As adults, very few of us know how to play; we must learn how. This is especially true of men. Without the skills of adult play, men play as if they were kids who never grew up. They get too silly, too competitive, too possessive. As you may remember, play is serious business to children.

He Doesn't Know How to Play

Having a man who knows how to play as an adult is important to your relationship. Unless your man (and you, too, don't forget) learns the guidelines to adult play, excess leisure time could easily create a tense atmosphere of hostility and grudge-holding.

The recommendations I'll make in this chapter will help you to teach your man a "play ethic" to go along with his work ethic. Without a play ethic, he falls victim to the pressure to approach play with the same dogged determination expected of him at work. Too many men end up so tense and exhausted from playing that they have to go back to work just to rest.

The following quiz will help you decide whether your man knows how to play. Answer yes or no to each question.

1. Does he laugh when he plays?
2. Does he not worry about what other people think of him when he's playing?
3. Does some of his play time include active playing with you?
4. Does he control his play (as opposed to being addicted to it)?
5. Can he still have fun if he loses in competitive play?

If you answered yes to all these questions, your man demonstrates a very positive play ethic. Each no suggests that he needs to learn how to play as an adult. If you answered no to four or five of the questions, your job will be very difficult. However, since play is an excellent stress reducer, teaching him to play could add years to his life.

I've outlined below the four principles of my play ethic. Also included are examples of what other women have done to help their men learn to play. Use your imagination and creativity to implement the play ethic any way you can. Obviously, you should first make sure that *you* know how to play by being able to answer yes to all the questions above.

1. *Learning how to play is as important as play itself.*

Your man takes a giant step toward accepting the necessity of developing a play ethic when he agrees that adult's play is different from child's play. Spontaneity is the crucial ingredient in learning how to play. A simple technique for increasing one's spontaneity is to create a story about a stranger.

The next time you and your man see a stranger on the street, make up a short story about the man, a story filled with intrigue, romance, and danger. Encourage your man to create a story about the next stranger you see.

2. *Play must be controlled; it must not control.*

Watching television is an example of passive play; and in and of itself, it is not bad. It's harmful only if there's no active play to balance it. When passive entertainment dominates active entertainment, addiction may result. And when addictive play becomes restrictive instead of freeing, tension-producing instead of relaxing, it interferes with, rather than promotes, the expression of love. If your man is addicted to television, try and introduce the habit of playing a challenging game once or twice a week (Trivial Pursuit, Scrabble, etc.).

3. *In competitive play, compete with yourself, not others.*

Competition is healthy for your man, provided that it's *intra*personal, that is, if he competes with himself by trying to improve upon his own past performance instead of trying to beat someone else. This type of "personal best" competition takes away the fierceness and pressure that too often result from interpersonal play. Urge your man to use performance charts to compare last week's performance to the current week's, monitoring such behavior as miles jogged, total tennis points scored, total golf putts, calories consumed, and laps swum.

4. *Your love partner must be included in some play.*

Playing is an important social event. It helps create new friendships and renew old ones. Although you certainly can't expect to share all the same recreational activities with your man, the two of you must reserve some time for playing together. It not only helps increase your friendship, but it also serves as an energizer for solving problems in other areas of your lives. In addition to the suggestions made above, taking leisurely walks, listening to music, dancing, and even watching television together are all examples of playing with your man.

Stress Is Killing Him

"Our doctor told my husband that he needs to learn how to relax," Nancy said. "But he doesn't know how. Even when he plays golf, he comes home all tensed up because he didn't have a good score."

Nancy, a forty-year-old woman with a heart of gold and hair to match, went on to explain that the only way Mark, her husband, could forget about a lousy golf game was to get back to the course as soon as possible and shoot another round. "Until he does that," she explained, "his bad score eats away at him like a disease."

"He sounds like so many other golfers," I said, remembering my own bout with my excessive drive to score well. "He doesn't 'play' golf, he 'works' golf. And it's maddening, because you can't *make* him relax."

Recommending Books

If, like Mark, your man "works" when he's supposed to be playing, try a simple program called *recommending books*. Talk with your local librarian and ask about publications from the American Management Association on stress management. If your spouse is a hard-driving businessman, it's likely that he'll pay more attention to an AMA publication than to one from another source. When you give him the book, be very general in your comments, saying, "I thought you might like to read this." Don't demand that he read the book or try to make him feel guilty if he doesn't.

Or try the spontaneity exercise referred to earlier. Spontaneity is the one thing that's missing from those men who don't know how to follow the doctor's orders and relax. Here's another example of a spontaneity exercise; it's a modified version of the word association test.

Spontaneity Exercise

The word association test—saying the first thing that comes into your mind—is supposed to tell a psychiatrist or psychologist something about your personality. In truth, the test is not nearly as reliable as other procedures. However, with a minor modification, it can become an excellent way to learn spontaneity.

The next time you're in the car together, suggest the "word association game" to pass the time. This is the way it works: you say a word and he must say the first word that comes into his mind; a brief, upbeat discussion can follow the query, "Where did that come from?" The modification is this: the word you say and his response must come from *two different chosen categories*. For example, your word could be something found around the house, and his word could be an animal.

Thus, you say, "doorknob," and he must respond with the

name of the first animal that comes to his mind. If you try it yourself, you'll realize that this is a tough game, calling for a bit of thoughtful spontaneity. You can, of course, change the categories to fit your special interests.

In playing this game, be careful not to analyze each other's responses. The game is intended to be a source of fun and laughter.

Nancy liked the thinking part of the game because Mark considered most games silly. "I think he'll do it," she said with a broad smile, "because it will challenge him to make a connection between a doorknob and a duck."

I Have to Be His Entertainment Committee

"Mark expects me to arrange all of our social activities," Nancy lamented later in our session. "If Saturday comes and I don't have an outing planned, he acts as if I've committed a sin. I'd feel guilty if I told him that I didn't want to be his entertainment committee."

Mark's job required that he entertain his colleagues, upper-level management people, and new clients. Nancy's problem with the social dimension of Mark's job was a bit more complicated than she had originally let on. A major source of the pressure she felt actually came from her feeling intimidated by some of the wives of his superiors, who she said acted as if they were better than her.

"It's getting so that I dread the weekends. I'm supposed to have a dinner party for eight and face women who scrutinize my every word and action. An hour or so before they're due to arrive, my nerves are on edge. By the time they get there, I'm convinced that I'm going to say something that will ruin Mark's chances in the company. I was shocked to learn how harshly executive's wives are judged by the other wives."

If you can identify with any part of Nancy's problem, you'll want to study two techniques, both of which will help you confront the situation as well as your man.

Balancing

If you're like most women, you don't mind being in charge of the social calendar. The problem arises when your man expects you to be in charge of whether or not he has a good time and you go along with it. If this shoe fits, then you need *balancing,* a form of cognitive restructuring (see page 38) in which you identify the limits of your responsibilities.

You should counterbalance your responsibility for social outings with the realization that you cannot make your husband have a good time. If you realize that he chooses to have fun or not, then you can stop being afraid of his disapproval and feeling guilty for causing his turmoil. Type or write, "I'm not responsible for my man having a good time," on a card; put it in the bathroom; and repeat it aloud several times a day for the next two weeks. Make sure you say it before you pick up the phone to make a dinner reservation for next Saturday night.

It may seem to you that you are excessively "internal," because you are bound and determined to figure out a way to use your socializing talents to control your husband's fun. However, in reality, you're operating from an external reference, believing that your husband doesn't have any responsibility for enjoying himself.

When you balance yourself, you're able to distinguish between what you can control and what you can't—what you can influence and to what degree. This is a lifelong process and one at which we always must work.

Negative Practice

A second technique is designed to help you deal with the intimidation coming from others at a social gathering. It's called *negative practice.* To accomplish it you must purposefully reproduce your symptoms of nervousness under conditions that you control. This is how it might work for you.

First, picture a situation that provokes anxiety in you; include your symptoms of nervousness. For example, think of meeting the president of the women's club and recall your trembling voice, shaky knees, and blank mind. Now, in the privacy of your own home, use behavioral rehearsal to recreate that moment. Force yourself to talk with a trembling voice as you pretend to say hello to the woman. Make your knees shake in a mock demonstration of this sign of anxiety. Practice saying something you consider to be stupid as if your mind were blank. Shrug your shoulders so that your neck is tight (possibly another symptom of which you're not aware).

You can expand negative practice to include other situations. Simply recall the particulars of the situation and picture yourself getting nervous. Then, do as you did above. When practicing, recreate the symptoms several times, giving yourself a minute or two of rest between each trial. If possible, practice throughout the day. If you complete the negative practice exercise once a day for two weeks, you should find some relief from your anxiety.

The logic behind this forceful recreation of anxiety symptoms is that the more you purposely produce the symptoms in a relatively peaceful situation, the greater your internal control over those symptoms. Keep in mind that negative practice does not address itself to feelings of inferiority. Therefore, you should protect yourself from such feelings with regular doses of self-acceptance (see Chapter 2).

Three Ways He Can Control His Competitiveness

Once Nancy gave herself permission to let Mark have a lousy time if he chose to, she used a modified version of *negative practice* to reduce her anxiety. (She learned to take the situation less seriously by practicing saying "dumb things" and realizing that she had more control over her actions than she gave herself credit for). With added self-confidence, she quit acting as if Mark's enjoyment was her responsibility. The more she ignored his sulking, the less he did it.

It was approximately four months later that this strategy paid Nancy even more dividends. Mark asked her for her advice on a problem, and she decided to get my opinion.

"Mark's competitiveness is getting him into trouble," she said, obviously confident about her ability to help her man. "His boss and a potential client came with their wives to our house for an informal cookout last Friday after work. Later on, we played Trivial Pursuit, and Mark was teamed with the client and the boss's wife. Well, he got so mad about losing that he started saying sarcastic things to everybody, his teammates included.

He was so upset that it dampened the party and people went home early.

"The next day, he felt terrible. He was embarrassed about the way he had acted in front of his boss and his wife, and worried about how his actions would be viewed. He asked me what he should do, and I didn't know what to tell him."

It's wonderful that Nancy was given the opportunity to be a consultant for her man. Such situations don't come along nearly often enough. However, if you ever have the chance to help your man control his competitiveness, there are three things you should remember to tell him.

- *Self-critique hierarchy.* In Chapter 7 (see page 100) I suggested that you apply this technique to yourself in order to demonstrate to your man how he might learn to overcome his fear of getting angry. Your man can use this same procedure to reverse a negative image that others may have of him.

  He should construct a hierarchy of self-criticisms, ranging from something that is fairly inconsequential ("I'm five pounds overweight") to a behavior that definitely needs improvement ("I procrastinate on doing my paperwork," or, "I have to learn how to relax and have fun"). Beginning at the bottom of the hierarchy, he should practice criticizing himself two or three times a day during informal interactions with his friends or coworkers. It would also be of great benefit if he constructed a self-critique hierarchy concerning his actions toward you and practiced it daily.

- *Positive self-referencing.* Positive self-referencing occurs when your man says aloud, "I'm a good person," or, "I'm a likable guy." In order for it to work, he must say it ten times a day for two weeks. If he's with others, he can say it to himself.

  The logic of this recommendation is simple: saying something positive about yourself will, at least temporarily, overcome any feelings of rejection or inadequacy.

- *Ego-control exercise.* The ego-control exercise is also simple. It works like this: a man competes with himself by seeing how long he can participate in a social conversation without using the words *I*, *me*, or *mine*, or making any other reference to himself. The exercise requires him to ask questions, make reflective comments, and generally interact as if what the other person is saying is more important than what he's thinking.

This exercise sensitizes him to the importance of controlling the overextension of his ego into conversations, and it makes him a nicer person to be around. Unfortunately, it also has the added effect of making people start confiding in him as if he were the resident shrink.

His Friends Drive Me Crazy

Gayle (she's the one who taught her man to throw his dirty exercise clothes in the washing machine) had such good luck with the strategic withdrawal program that I suggested she modify it for use on another problem.

"I have a hard time liking Keith's friends," she explained, "especially two of his regular tennis partners. One guy is a womanizer and the other one drinks too much. I don't like to be around them. But when they come to our house, Keith expects me to serve a snack. I really don't mind doing that for most of his friends, but not these two guys."

Many couples get themselves into trouble by trying to share everything. This can be tough when it comes to friends. His friends don't have to be yours, and vice versa.

If Gayle's complaint rings a bell for you, do what she did. She first decided whether or not the rift over friends represented a deeper problem in her relationship. You can make that decision by examining two key traits in your relationship—commitment and emotional intimacy. Do that by reading each of the following statements and deciding how often your man does each one. You needn't assign a score to each statement.

Ignores me when I need to talk.
Tells other people my secrets.
Keeps bringing up my past mistakes.

Makes subtle threats of leaving me.

Rarely, if ever, tells me his feelings.

Doesn't say, "I love you," unless I badger him.

Seems indifferent to my hurts and joys.

Pretends to be perfect.

If any of these things occurs often, you should consider the possibility that the conflict over friends is actually a symptom of other, more complicated problems. If this is the case, consult other sections of this book (Chapter 11, Handling His Insensitivity, and Chapter 12, Stopping His Mental Abuse).

If things really are fine except for not liking his friends, employ a modified version of the *strategic withdrawal program* (page 143).

Keep direct contact with the friends to a minimum. When you must spend time with his friends, use cognitive restructuring to tell yourself, "Being with these people for the next hour is the price I have to pay to enjoy a loving relationship."

Continue the program by gradually reducing your part of the conversation. Also, find activities that will please your man while minimizing contact with his friends (make an elaborate snack for them that requires you to spend time at the store and in the kitchen). Or schedule an activity that takes you away from the house when his friend is there. (This is another example of the stimulus-control program; see page 96). Or, finally, make yourself busy in another room reading.

Admit your dislike without making a big deal out of it or attacking your man. "I don't like that guy, but if you do, that's okay. I just don't want to be around him unless I have to. So if you see me withdrawing, you'll understand." Do not argue over whether or not your dislike is justified.

If the conflict over friends is intense and frequent but you can't clearly identify another, more complicated relationship problem, you probably could benefit from a session or two with a professional counselor.

Working at building a pleasurable social life is very important to the success of your relationship. Learning to play together can rekindle the old flames of romance that were present during the early days. Unfortunately, the hurry-up-and-be-happy approach to life can often blur the fact that, when all is said and done, laughter *is* the best medicine.

15.

MANAGING SPECIAL
PROBLEMS

The women you are about to meet—Helen, Marion, and Susan—all endured mental abuse from their men, who were insensitive and volatile. However, each woman faced a special problem that made confronting her man particularly difficult. Helen's husband was depressed; Marion's was an alcoholic; and Susan's man was so unsupportive that her own fears blossomed into a problem that made it impossible for her to enjoy a normal life.

Each woman believed that her relationship had a future, and each one sought professional help to try and reach that future. All three of these women's men were unwilling to come along for counseling.

I'm Afraid of My Own Shadow

"I'm an agoraphobiac," forty-year-old Susan told me with shame in her voice. "In my case it means that I have a difficult time leaving my house even to do the simplest task. Ted and I have many friends who want to get together on weekends. But I just can't go. I tell Ted to go without me, but he's getting tired of making excuses for me. My problem is a source of constant tension between us."

"Have you sought help before now?" I asked.

"Yes, I've been seeing a counselor for several months."

"What do you talk about?"

"Mostly about my childhood fears and my relationship with my mother."

"Why have you decided to see me?"

"Because my fears are not getting better; in fact, they're getting worse."

I carefully reviewed Susan's symptoms, her relationship with Ted, and her counseling experience. It was clear that she was experiencing a great deal of free-floating anxiety. It was also clear that talking about the past was doing very little to help her with the present. But it wasn't until she talked about doing her weekly shopping that she revealed a major contributor to her phobia.

"It's very difficult for me to go grocery shopping," she said. "My favorite grocery store is about two miles away and I have to cross a bridge over an expressway to get there. So I drive about five miles out of my way to get to the store without crossing that bridge."

"What happens when you cross the bridge?" I asked.

"I panic. I look down at the expressway and realize there's nothing supporting me, that I could fall at any moment."

Hearing the words "nothing supporting me," I immediately launched into a careful analysis of Susan's relationship with Ted. More than one clinical study has concluded that husbands of agoraphobiacs are typically unsupportive of their wives, and this lack of support is often symbolically expressed when the woman is deathly afraid to cross bridges and other spanning structures.

Susan's man didn't help her with the household chores, rarely shared his feelings with her, and reacted to her phobia by saying, "Why don't you just do what you have to do?" While Ted was essentially a nice guy, his understanding of Susan's condition was woefully insufficient.

"I don't blame Ted for my condition," Susan said, obviously feeling she had gone too far in criticizing her man. "It's my problem, not his."

"And I wholeheartedly agree," I countered. "To think other-

174

wise is to put yourself in a prison from which you can't escape. But Ted's lack of support *contributes* to your phobia. You'll have a much easier time conquering it if you don't have to face it alone."

"How can he help me?" she asked sincerely.

"You'll have to teach him how, but first *you* must determine what you need. It's your responsibility to gather the latest psychological and medical information concerning the treatment of your condition, find the people to assist you in your treatment, and then teach your man how to help you, even confronting him in a loving way if you must."

In Vivo Desensitization

I then outlined for Susan the latest behavioral treatment for agoraphobia, a treatment that shows great promise. It is called *in vivo* desensitization, a daily, reality-based exercise lasting several weeks or months, in which a person takes small steps in conquering a fear. The key element of this treatment is the development of an individualized fear hierarchy—a list of five or six situations ranked from the least to the most frightening.

Here's how *in vivo* desensitization would work with a hypothetical fear. Let's say you are single and the man you love is an urban cowboy. You want to learn to share his love of riding horses. Let's also say, however, that horses terrify you.

First, you'd think of six or seven interactions between you and a horse and rank them from the least to the most frightening. Here's a sample list:

Watching a movie of Roy Rogers and Trigger, a truly wonderful horse.

Going to a stable, standing one hundred feet away, and watching a friendly horse.

Standing nearby as your lover rides a friendly horse.

Patting a friendly horse.

Sitting on a friendly horse.

Riding a friendly horse.

The goal of the treatment would be for you to become comfortable with each item on your list before moving on to the next one. Therefore, before going out to the stable, you'd watch Trigger on TV without getting upset. It's important to be relaxed during each small step as well as to give yourself positive thoughts—*i.e.*, "I won't get hurt if I learn to ride slowly and with people I trust."

Although it's not absolutely necessary, it would be helpful if your lover was with you during each phase of your desensitization to give you support and encouragement about horses; for example, he could say, "All the horses I ride are gentle." Depending upon your motivation and your level of fear, you could be "tall in the saddle" in as short a time as a few weeks.

In vivo desensitization helps you solve a specific problem in a real-life situation. The treatment can be effective even if there are other, more complex reasons for your fear (for example, you fear social gatherings because you've not yet resolved your feelings of being rejected during junior high school). You needn't resolve all past conflicts (that's unrealistic) in order to improve the quality of your daily life.

While research indicates that self-directed desensitization can be successful, it's also clear that it's even more successful if supervised by a therapist experienced in the treatment. If you have trouble with any part of the procedure, call a psychologist, a referral service, a hospital's behavioral medicine department, or a university psychology clinic in order to find someone who can supervise your treatment.

In Susan's particular case, she found a behavioral therapist who guided her through a desensitization program and talked with her about leftover angry thoughts about her childhood. Ted understood enough about her condition not to make fun of it and occasionally helped her with a step in her hierarchy. The last time I heard from her, she was able to go to the grocery store over the bridge. However, she still wasn't thrilled about it.

When He's Depressed

"Nothing seems to please him," Helen said about her husband Roger. "He complains about the neighbor's dog, and he used to love it; he sits in front of the television and sleeps, and he's lost interest in playing golf. I'd say our sex life is bad, but we don't even have one. The last time I tried to hold his hand he accused me of being a sex maniac. That's not like the Roger I knew."

It didn't take long to determine that Roger was experiencing a mild to moderate depression. He was irritable (the complaints), withdrawing from things he used to like (friends and golf), and had lost interest in sex. His sleeping during the day was also an indication of depression (as is any change in sleeping or eating habits). Roger was eating well, seemed to enjoy his work, and made no references to ending his life. If there had been disturbance in these areas as well, his depression would have been severe and Helen would have had to take more direct action (such as taking him to a depression clinic or hospital). As it was, I suggested she try the *depression program* before taking any stronger action.

Depression Program

Research has shown that although depressed partners talk about themselves and their future negatively, they usually "put on a happy face" around their friends. So if you think your man isn't depressed because he's friendly toward other people, he may just be covering up his feelings.

He may resist your efforts at first, but use a tender toughness to confront him with the facts of his situation.

The first step in the depression program is to conduct a brief analysis of recent behavior, much as I did with Helen. Has his behavior recently changed dramatically? Is he withdrawing from activities he used to enjoy? Is he more irritable or restless? Is he experiencing eating or sleeping disturbances? Does he have crying spells? Does he make any references to suicide or being "too tired to go on"? Has his ability to concentrate or make decisions deteriorated? Each yes contributes to the possibility of depression.

If you're uncertain as to the severity of the depression, suspend the depression program and contact a depression clinic, or seek a referral from your family doctor, clergyperson, or other reliable source.

When calling for an appointment, ask the doctor if he or she is familiar with the use of cognitive therapy in the treatment of depression. Research demonstrates that cognitive therapy is just as good as, and sometimes better than, drug therapy. The advantage of going to a clinic is that you are likely to find several approaches to treatment, including the evaluation of possible medical complications.

If the self-help depression program seems adequate, here are other recommendations for you to use in helping your man (or yourself):

MOVE YOUR BODY. Some type of exercise (*e.g.*, walking) increases production of the hormone norepinephrine, which is associated with reduced depression.

ACHIEVE A GOAL. Clean a cupboard, mow the lawn, wash the floor, wax the car, or do anything, however small, that gives you a sense of achievement. The achievement helps counteract the automatic thought, "I'm a total failure," while it keeps the body in motion.

DISTRACT YOURSELF. You shouldn't force yourself to solve problems while you're depressed. Find activities that will distract you from thinking about yourself.

COUNTERACT IRRATIONAL THOUGHTS. Depressed people believe such things as, "I can't do anything right," "Nobody likes me," and, "There's no hope for change." These thoughts should be restructured with rational alternatives: "Making mistakes only proves I'm human," "I'm likable just the way I am," and, "I change every minute whether I like it or not." Dr. David Burns's book, *Feeling Good: The New Mood Therapy,* is an excellent source of self-help for counteracting irrational thoughts.

He's an Alcoholic

"I realize he's an alcoholic," Marion said sadly. "After ten years of denial, I've been forced to face the truth. He still denies it, but even his best friend knows something is wrong. He has several drinks almost every night, and when he drinks his personality changes. He gets drunk once or twice a month, he drinks instead of talking about his troubles at work, and if I say anything, he brags that he could quit anytime he wanted to."

Alcohol Program

There's no tougher confrontation than the one that the spouse of an alcoholic must make. The following *alcohol program* is designed to minimize pain for the family members of an alcoholic and maximize the chances that he or she will seek treatment. Its key feature is that it gives you something constructive to do short of leaving the relationship. As most people soon realize, you can not *save* a loved one from his own alcoholism.

REINFORCE HIM WHEN HE'S NOT DRINKING. Fix his favorite foods, initiate sex, and energetically participate in activities he enjoys.

ENCOURAGE COMPETING ACTIVITIES. Taking the kids on a picnic, joining new organizations that feature nondrinking activities, and socializing with nondrinking friends are a few of the activities you can arrange or encourage that directly compete with other, drinking-related activities.

FIND OUTSIDE ACTIVITIES. The partner of an alcoholic should find activities that eliminate those situations in which old caretaking habits are likely to resurface (for example, preparing dinner for him when you know he's drinking). Review the stimulus-control program (see page 96).

GAIN SUPPORT. Participate actively in some type of support group. Women Helping Women, Al-Anon, and church groups offer encouragement and guidance.

IGNORE HIM OR HER WHEN HE OR SHE IS DRINKING. Refrain from arguing with or trying to take liquor away from your partner; do not bail him or her out of a sticky situation.

PREVENT ABUSE. A woman should take steps to identify the cues that are likely to lead to abuse, whether physical or emotional.

Listen for "drunk sounds" (*e.g.*, slamming the door, a loud voice) and look for other changes in behavior signifying alcohol abuse.

You (and your children, if any) should prearrange with a friend, relative, or someone from a women's center to stay overnight. If you are unable to ignore him, take the children and leave. If he's violent, do not tell him of this plan in advance; if he isn't violent, explain that you don't want to be around him when he's drinking.

EXERT PEER PRESSURE. Organizations have found that surrounding an alcoholic with friends, family, and coworkers who together confront the person with his or her alcoholic behavior can have an impact on willingness to seek treatment.

In addition to this program, I suggest you visit an alcohol treatment center. A certified alcoholism counselor can help you implement these and other recommendations.

16.

CONFRONTING YOUR NEW LOVER

The earlier a problem in a relationship is confronted, the better. You'll recall the *quid pro quo* concept that says the rules of a relationship are established early—a few of them probably during your first date. Since most of these rules are unspoken, it's important to identify harmful ones as soon as possible. The earlier you confront your new lover, the more you can be assured that the confrontation will be a loving one.

Up to now we've looked at issues within established relationships. Now let's examine some important matters having to do with couples who have just gotten started.

When You're Worried the Relationship Might Fail

Twenty-seven-year-old Debbie was engaged to marry thirty-year-old Carey. She loved him but was so anxious about making her marriage work that she was having second thoughts.

"I'm worried about getting married," Debbie told me. "I've never admitted it out loud, but I'm afraid my marriage will end up in divorce court like so many others. I wish there was such a thing as a marriage guarantee."

"What exactly are you worried about?" I asked.

"I don't know, maybe nothing," she answered. "Carey and I love each other, and we get along fine. It's just that . . . well, sometimes he gets his mind made up and nothing I say seems to make any difference."

"For example?"

"For example, going to his parents' house every Sunday. He did it before we met, we do it now, and he sees nothing wrong with doing it after we're married."

"But . . . ?"

"But I want us to develop our own home, our own special routine."

It was obvious that Carey's attachment to his parents would not stop Debbie from marrying him. However, she needed something to help her confront the problem that loomed on the horizon of their love. There is help for those who face a relationship conflict for the first time and are worried about confronting it without generating bad feelings. It's what I call the *new lover's conflict resolution program* (NLCRP).

The New Lover's Conflict Resolution Program

The NLCRP is designed to be used the moment you have your first conflict; and as I'm sure you know, that moment comes long before the wedding or your first night in the same apartment. The NLCRP can also be used by love partners who've been through plenty of conflict but would like to find a fresh way to resolve disagreements.

The NLCRP has three steps that, when implemented as outlined, will permit you to resolve conflicts quickly and sensibly.

1. GET THE ISSUES OUT IN THE OPEN. Because you fear being selfish, insensitive, or disloyal, you may fail to make your desires known. However, the NLCRP can't work unless both of you get the issues that are important to you out in the open. If you don't, you'll eventually begin to replace your desires with destructive criticisms.

2. ACTIVELY DISCUSS THE ISSUES. The goal of a lively discussion is for both partners to understand the other's perspective on the problem. If one or both of you have not gotten the issues out in the open, a rational discussion is impossible. Instead, hostile and caustic nonverbal gestures begin to characterize your interaction.

3. NEGOTIATE THE MOST CRITICAL ISSUES. The idea of *quid pro quo* (see page 157) can be used to stimulate a compromise. Yield to your partner on an issue critical to him, provided he vows to reciprocate. You know that negotiation has broken down when one or both of you continue to press for concessions that are clearly inappropriate or to push for solutions that have already been rejected.

Debbie was able to employ the NLCRP to resolve the conflict over spending every Sunday at Carey's parents'. She was able to get the issues out in the open and discuss them by making it *very* clear that a compromise had to be reached. It was critically important that Debbie stated her feelings and goals logically and without undue emotion. The morning after their discussion, Carey reluctantly admitted that he, too, would like to stop seeing his parents every Sunday, but that he felt guilty about wanting to do so.

After weighing the alternatives and discussing their feelings, Debbie and Carey reached a compromise in which they used strategic withdrawal (see page 143) to reduce the visits to a manageable few while minimizing guilt and discomfort.

They agreed that beginning with the coming Sunday, they would leave his parents' home fifteen minutes sooner than they had the week before. They further agreed that after four Sundays, they would skip a Sunday. Their goal was to reach a point where they would visit his parents every six or seven weeks. During this weaning process, Debbie agreed to call Carey's parents after each visit to express her thanks for their hospitality.

If you have a conflict to resolve with your lover, check your implementation of the NLCRP by answering these questions:

STAGE 1

Do you support each other's feelings about your respective disagreements?

Do you refrain from interrupting each other?

Do you tolerate the other being upset?

Do you understand each other's feelings fairly quickly?

Your answers to these questions should be "frequently" or "almost always."

STAGE 2

Can you identify the specific areas of disagreement?

Can you identify the specific areas of agreement?

Can you express your partner's viewpoint nearly as well as your own?

Do the facial expressions or tones of voice of either of you convey bitterness, anger, disgust, condescension, hostility, resentment, cynicism, or self-pity?

The answers to the first three questions should be "frequently" or "almost always"; the fourth question should be answered "never" or "once in a while."

STAGE 3

Does either of you try to change your agreement after you've reached a compromise?

Do you reargue later on?

Do you end up with very little resolved after all?

Does either of you keep proposing things that are not mutually acceptable?

The answers to these questions should all be "never" or "once in a while." Each wrong answer can lead to conflict resolution if you simply rephrase the question into a statement of proposed action and implement it the next time you use the NLCRP.

184

If the NLCRP is carefully applied during the first few conflicts, it will become habitual and eventually lead to the resolution of conflicts before they have a chance to create any estrangement between you and your man.

Confronting Him for the First Time

"Jake and I have always had a pretty smooth relationship," Judy said, tugging at her thick black hair in frustration. "But recently there's been a storm cloud over our love. It's his jealousy and possessiveness. Our relationship is serious but not binding—just exactly where we both want it."

"Give me a typical situation," I said.

"I work, take care of my two kids from my first marriage, run a house, and make time for Jake. I also try to make time for myself. But if I'm not right there waiting for him when he gets to my house, he acts as if I had committed a crime."

"What does he say?"

"Well, the other day I was talking to my neighbor when Jake pulled into my driveway. I said 'hi,' and came into the house soon after he walked inside. As I walked in, he said, 'Did you have a good time with Marcie the mouth?' I'm never sure what to say when he gets that way. Once he said, 'You never treat me as if I'm special; I feel as if I'm just another one of your good friends.' "

I warned Judy not to get caught up in analyzing her man's inner fears. Not only would her analysis fail, but she would also be playing the role of Jake's counselor—an absolutely disastrous role for any woman to play with a man (and vice versa).

If you see a problem in your new relationship—for example, jealousy or possessiveness—and want to confront it, here are guidelines you should follow to insure that the confrontation is loving and will get you started on the right foot.

- *Evaluate your level of sexism.* Many women are surprised to find that their first loving confrontation brings them face to face with their own sexist attitudes. These questions will help you evaluate any sexism you might have: Do you believe

185

that men are unable to handle their own emotions? Do you think a man's feelings are more easily hurt than a woman's? Do you back away from confronting a man because you're afraid he will reject you, because a man's ego can't handle being confronted by a woman?

- *Confront your sexism.* Confront any sexism you've found in your attitudes. The following ideas will help you change your attitudes: The male ego may be weaker in some respects, but it's far from being fragile. Men can handle their own emotions, it just may take some time. Just because men aren't as emotionally open as women doesn't mean they can't learn. An excellent way for a man to learn is to be confronted in a loving way by his woman.

- *Confront your man as soon as possible.* The first time you see something that bothers you, make a mental note of it, then let it pass. However, if it happens again in a relatively short period of time (a week or two), confront him. The sooner you confront your man, the more likely you are to do it in a gentle, loving way.

- *Put the responsibility on him.* If the problem you wish to confront involves your man's complaint about you (as was true for Jake and Judy), don't assume you know what he wants. Put the responsibility on him by saying, "What do you want from me?" or, "Tell me exactly what you would like me to do."

- *Control your emotions.* Make your confrontation free from cynicism, sarcasm, and other negative emotions. If you can't control your emotions, don't confront him.

- *Make your request crystal clear.* If the problem involves something you want from him, use denominalization (see page 106) to keep your request behavioral. Use the basic communication script (see page 80) to guide you if you get confused. "When you do or say ————, I feel ————. My request is that you ————."

- *Keep your request positive.* Do not tell your man which behavior you want him to stop; instead, tell him the behavior you want him to *begin.* Do not say, "My request is that you quit being nasty to me." Say, "My request is that you say something nice to me before being critical."

- *Let the little things pass.* Many new lovers get themselves into trouble by trying to solve, or at least discuss, every little problem that comes up. There are many minor disagreements (where to eat lunch, which movie to see, whether to have pot roast or pizza) that are best left to pass on into oblivion.
- *Confront the fear of rejection.* If you're afraid of rejection, remind yourself that what you feel now is probably worse than what you'll feel after a loving confrontation.

Do I Want a Commitment Right Now?

"Tad's pushing me to get married," twenty-nine-year-old Jill explained. "But I'm not sure I'm ready. I think he's the guy for me, but I need more time. My first marriage didn't work out too well, and I don't want to rush into another one without being more sure of my future. I also want to have kids and don't want a divorce messing them up.

"Tad says my divorce is still affecting me, that I'm afraid of commitment. I never thought of it that way, but maybe he's right."

"Do you love him?" I asked.

"Yes, I do," Jill said matter-of-factly, "but that's not enough, not this time anyway. I want to know that we can solve our problems, and that takes time."

"Do you and Tad have problems now?"

"Not really," she replied. "That's what's so confusing. We get along great, except when he starts pressing me to get married. I don't know what to say."

There were two possible explanations of Jill's problem: (1) She loved Tad and wanted to marry him eventually but was resisting because of her fear of commitment. If so, she needed to confront herself before confronting Tad. (2) She simply was not ready to make the necessary commitment. If so, she needed to confront Tad's persistence as soon as possible.

Prolonged Exposure

If you're not certain whether or not to confront your new lover, delay the confrontation in favor of gaining greater self-understanding. You can use the technique of *prolonged exposure* to decide whether your current relationship has long-term potential. If it does, you'll want to invest the time and energy it takes for a successful confrontation.

The goal of prolonged exposure is to project a long-term commitment with all its attendant payoffs and pitfalls and see how you like it. Here's what to do:

Deeply relax (see Chapter 5) twice daily. After inducing a peaceful feeling, picture the latest man in your life moving in with you. See the boxes, the changes in your closet, and imagine the upset of your daily routine. Note your feelings when imagining these things.

Then, imagine the companionship on lonely nights, the sharing of good and bad days at work, and the warmth of spending holidays with someone you love. Note the feelings associated with these images.

Continue this procedure daily for at least two weeks. Write down your reactions in two columns, marked "positive" and "negative," representing the good and bad feelings you had during your sessions. It's important to complete the exercise every day—the more prolonged the exercise, the more reliable the emotional data generated.

If your negative feelings outweigh your positive ones, it probably confirms that you don't want a commitment, for whatever reason. If those negative feelings center on fear and apprehension, it may indicate the presence of insecurity. If they reflect boredom or inconvenience, this man may not be the right one for you.

If you conclude that you're afraid of commitment, you can use prolonged exposure to help you to confront that fear, which will in turn better enable you to confront your man. Follow these steps:

1. Continue deep relaxation daily. Start imagining your man moving into your bedroom in a permanent manner.

2. Imagine that he says he doesn't love you, or that he wants to leave you, or that you don't satisfy him. Make the image of rejection as real as possible—for example, have him sitting in the living room, perhaps slightly inebriated. Hear him say the words that you fear hearing the most ("You don't satisfy me").

3. Say this or a similar cognitive restructuring thought aloud: "I'm a loving person, and if he rejects me, it's *his* fault, not mine." Continue breathing deeply and relaxing. Repeat the new thought several times.

Whenever you employ the prolonged exposure technique, it's critically important to remember these rules: if you're unable to deeply relax or harness your imagination (check the imagination test in Chapter 5), do not attempt this technique until you've improved your imagery powers. If the images turn so negative that you're unable to continue deep relaxation, stop immediately and try again later. Never push the exercise if you're not in control of it.

As so often happens, Jill applied the prolonged exposure technique in a manner we had not discussed. She told Tad that she wasn't sure why she withdrew from him when he pushed to get married. She explained the concept of prolonged exposure in such a way that Tad decided to do it with her. After two weeks of daily practice, Jill decided she simply wasn't ready for marriage. Surprisingly, *so did Tad.* He quit pushing her to get married.

17.
SURVIVING
THE END OF LOVE

If you've accepted your role as a teacher, then you've also accepted the fact that your man, as a student, has the right to refuse your lessons. If your man refuses to change after you've adapted my recommendations to your situation and confronted him in several different ways over a period of at least several months, then there's an excellent chance that the commitment you once made to each other is gone.

How Do I Know If It's Over?

Commitment is the glue that keeps a relationship together. It is, however, a concept over which partners disagree. He may say it means bringing home a good paycheck, while you say it means sharing intimate secrets. In the final analysis, if he doesn't change his viewpoint and learn how to dig deeper into himself and share something more than his money and possessions, you'll be forced to face, and survive, the end of love.

But when have you reached that point of no return? There's no absolute answer—another fact with which you'll have to live. You can only make the best determination with the least chance for error that is humanly possible.

190

Here are three procedures you can use to shed an objective light on the question, "Is it over?"

COMMITMENT TEST. You can examine your current commitment by answering yes or no to the following ten questions. Chances are you're going to want to say yes to each question if for no other reason than to add hope to a distressing situation. So be honest with yourself.

Does he *voluntarily* leave social outings to come home (as opposed to feeling he must report in)?

Does he share weaknesses about himself with you?

Does he still appreciate you when you have an unkempt appearance?

Do you enjoy your sex life with him?

When you lovingly confront him, do you feel that he has recognized your complaint?

Is he willing to adjust his behavior to the changing needs of your relationship?

Does he encourage you to have interests that might take you away from him (as opposed to being jealous of your outside interests)?

Is he *constructively* critical of you and your problems?

Will he tolerate inconvenience in order to help you?

Do you *firmly* believe that you'll be together five years from now (barring death)?

Add up your yes answers and you'll have an indication of your commitment on a 10-point scale. If you're an 8 or better, it doesn't appear that you need to ask the question, "Is it over?" If you're a 5 or above, you have work to do, but there seems to be reason for hope. If you're below a 5, your commitment is shaky and your relationship is likely to need major repairs.

BEHAVIORAL QUOTIENT (BQ). In calculating the BQ of your relationship, list ten interactions you've had with your man in the recent past. An interaction is anything from a simple kiss or an exchange of greetings to an intense hour-long conversation. (If you can't recall ten, keep a log for the next day or two until your list numbers ten.) Now, next to the word or phrase representing each interaction, put a + or a −, signifying whether the overall interaction was positive or negative in your view.

The number of positive interactions out of ten is the behavioral quotient of your relationship. If this quotient is 7 or more, you and your partner are quite compatible. If your quotient is 5 or 6, you have the foundation for improving your relationship and should continue working at it. If only three or four of the interactions are positive, then your relationship may be in need of professional help. If your quotient is 0, 1, or 2, your future together doesn't look good.

EMOTIONAL QUOTIENT (EQ). The EQ is less exact than the BQ. You calculate it by looking at a photo album from earlier, and perhaps happier, days. Find a picture that represents a pleasant outing (a family picnic, a vacation). If you have trouble finding such a picture, look at the pictures of your wedding. Then ask yourself: Is there any part of me that still feels the warmth and love associated with those days? To what degree?

Give your positive feeling a ranking from 1 to 10, with 10 representing a very warm and pleasant feeling. That number represents the EQ of your relationship.

Your commitment score and behavioral and emotional quotients give you as much objective information as you can collect without the help of a professional counselor. (If you're sincerely asking, "Is it over?" you should be talking to a professional.) However, *do not* rely upon any counselor to be your only source of objective information. Again I remind you: *you are your own best therapist.*

Once you've gathered the information, I urge you to set the results aside for a week and then repeat the procedure at least once more. If you're in the difficult position of asking, "Is it over?" you must give your mind and heart time to weigh the answers you generate. Your interpretation of the data may change from one week to the next. So please—*go slowly!*

Making the Last-Ditch Effort

If you'll recall, Julie (you met her in the introduction) had more than one simple problem to confront. Her husband said he loved her, but she felt he rarely showed it. She had been asking, "Is it over?" for several months. Her commitment score was 4, the BQ of her relationship was 3, and her EQ was so low that she wasn't able to give it a number. Yet, as you also remember, she wasn't ready to give up.

Julie believed that she had been too bitchy and indirect in past confrontations. She wanted to improve her teaching skills before saying, "Yes, it's over."

"One of my biggest problems," Julie said honestly, "is asking for what I want. If I have to ask for a hug, or for him to listen to me, or even for help with the dishes, there's this side of me that rebels. It says, 'If Andy really loved me, he'd do these things without my asking.' "

"But," I countered, "you can't expect him to be a mind reader."

"I know," she responded sincerely. "I'm just telling you how I feel."

Julie's feeling is evidence of a condition called *frozen spontaneity*. When spontaneity is frozen, love partners refuse to listen to each other or to try new approaches to old problems. Frozen spontaneity is probably the most frequent roadblock to solving relationship problems.

Spontaneity can only be thawed if the real feeling behind the complaint, "I don't feel appreciated," is discussed. However, such a discussion is usually thwarted because each partner believes that the other has ill will; that is, the feeling, "He really wants to see me suffer," or, "She really doesn't love me."

If you believe your man has ill will toward you and your relationship, you face a last-ditch situation. I suggest that you write him a letter covering these points:

Your marriage is in serious trouble and may not survive.

Though frustrated, you're not ready to give up.

You don't feel appreciated.

You request that he join you in a special analysis of your relationship.

RELATIONSHIP-VALUE ANALYSIS. While you can complete the commitment test, the BQ, and the EQ by yourself, you must conduct the relationship-value analysis with your man. This analysis focuses on the five factors that cause divorce. Obviously, you don't have to be in a last-ditch situation to complete the analysis. (All couples could complete the analysis on a yearly basis in order to "divorce-proof" their relationship.) This analysis might help you and your man overcome the ill will that may be standing between you and a renewed relationship.

You and your man should state your position on each of the values below, identify the area(s) of greatest discrepancy, and through discussion determine whether either of you would be willing to adjust your attitude in order to close the gap between you.

Allow at least an hour for your analysis and discussion. Take turns reading my remarks aloud, and then use a number between 1 and 10 to answer each question. (Use the examples to guide your judgment). If for any reason you get into an argument, suspend the analysis and try it again later.

SEXUAL FIDELITY. Sexual faithfulness can fall victim to the "sell-it-with-sex" approach of today's society. What's your current position on the importance of sexual fidelity within your relationship? Examples: 1 = "You can hop in bed anytime you get a chance"; 4 = "It's basically okay, but I don't want to know"; 7 = "I'll survive, but I'll hate it"; 10 = "If you're unfaithful, our relationship is over."

MONEY. The romantic notion of, "I can live on love," can within months become, "I need more spending money." At this point in your relationship, how important is money? Examples: 1 = "I can still live on love"; 4 = "Love is still the most important, but I could use an extra ten dollars a week"; 7 = "Our love life would suffer without enough money"; 10 = "I can always buy my way to more love, but I can't love my way to more money."

SACRIFICE/PLEASURE. Many couples get into serious conflict over the relative importance of sacrificing for long-term goals versus enjoying short-term pleasure. Where do you place yourself on this sacrifice/pleasure continuum? Examples: 1 = "I'll gladly forego anything if I know my later years are protected"; 4 = "I'll enjoy today only if I know it won't hurt me tomorrow"; 7 = "Sacrifice is fine but it shouldn't hurt"; 10 = "To hell with the mortgage, I'm going skiing."

EXCELLENCE/MEDIOCRITY. Arguments over standards of excellence can erode a relationship without either partner realizing it. How important is excellence to you? Examples: 1 = "I try not to let excellence interfere with my life"; 4 = "I've always tried to be average"; 7 = "I want things to be excellent, but imperfection won't ruin my life"; 10 = "If it's not done perfectly, then it really isn't done."

PHYSICAL ATTRACTIVENESS. A neat, well-kept appearance is very important to many people. How important is it to you? Examples: 1 = "Love doesn't care how it's packaged"; 4 = "I can love anyone unless he or she looks and smells like an old truck"; 7 = "It's easier to love someone who's attractive"; 10 = "Love means always looking good for your partner."

There really isn't a "correct" score for this analysis. It's most important that you and your man's respective scores not be too far apart on any one factor. If you're a 10 on sexual fidelity and he's a 3, your relationship's in trouble. If you're a 4 on the excellence/mediocrity factor and he's a 10, you will both have to give a little to make your love work. I usually recommend that couples shoot for an average of 6 or 7.

LAST-DITCH EFFORT. If your man rejects this analysis, there's only one thing left for you to do. The *last-ditch program* requires that you suspend all other programs and techniques and implement the following six recommendations (which can, by the way, be used effectively in other than last-ditch situations):

PLEASURING. Spend at least one day using the pleasuring technique discussed at the end of Chapter 7, Coping with His Temper. If you've already tried it, do it again.

LETTER. Write him a letter restating the three or four problems in your relationship that must be changed. Use denominalization (see page 106) to make your complaints clear and concise. Tell him this is your last attempt.

ANCHORING. This technique consists of recalling a positive emotion you felt for your man—warmth, tenderness, appreciation—and then intentionally recalling it several times a day. The more often you anchor yourself with a positive memory, the greater your chances of communicating with your man without an edge of suspiciousness or insecurity. If you don't get a kind word or action in return, you'll probably drop your anchor within a day or two.

ACTIVE REMINISCENCE. Pull out pictures of your courting days or your wedding, make a list of the activities you enjoyed at that time, and then suggest to your man that you do one of those things during the coming weekend. Picnicking, boating, movies, and dancing could all be activities from the past that would help you know your man better today. Again, if you don't receive a positive response from him within a few days, active reminiscence will quickly fade away.

POSITIVE SELF-REFERENCING. Type or print some positive comments about yourself on a card and put it on your bathroom mirror. "I'm a terrific woman," "I'm doing the best job of loving that I possibly can," and, "My love could move a mountain *if* the mountain wanted to move," are examples of overt self-instructions that when said aloud, ten times a day, will help you love yourself at a time when you may not feel too lovable.

SELF-OBSERVATION. Identify at least one attitude or attribute you've changed during the process of trying to teach your man to change (for example, becoming an "internal" woman, controlling your bitterness, solving problems in a direct, rational manner). Remind yourself of this growth when you're tempted to say that the past has been wasted.

If, after several weeks, you still see no change in your man's behavior, then you are forced to say, "Yes, it's over." (I again suggest that you consult a professional before closing the door on a relationship.)

Once you've made the decision, I strongly encourage you to use one last overt self-instruction. Type or print on a card, "I'm not the dealer." This is in reference to the analogy presented in the introduction to the book, in which I referred to a relationship as a card game and warned you of the pitfall of trying to change your man by dealing him a new hand of cards.

What If I Have to Get a Divorce?

Although they might not want to admit it, women often have thoughts about getting a divorce—especially women who were married before the age of twenty, have preschool-age children, have a desire for a career, or have a man who won't change.

If you face the possibility of divorce, you'll need reliable information. Keep in mind the following:

- A newly divorced woman typically has difficulty

    talking to a former spouse about money
    talking to a former spouse about children
    talking with a child about her life
    dating new people
    developing an intimate relationship
    overcoming depression
    overcoming loneliness
    making ends meet

- A newly divorced woman should seek help with single parenting (if applicable), legal and financial concerns, career

197

planning, socialization, and housing and homemaking. Those who seek help suffer significantly less than those who attempt to see it through alone.
- Not having enough money, guilt and self-blame, difficulty concentrating, and psychological problems are a divorced woman's biggest hurdles in the first six months.
- Sexual dissatisfaction is low at first, then increases, and then gradually goes back down.
- A newly divorced woman should concentrate on the following areas:

> improving her financial position
> dating
> developing intimate relationships
> going to school
> learning new things about herself
> accepting and redirecting angry thoughts
> talking with others who are divorced
> establishing a new life for herself
> taking care of her home

Although divorce is a stressful event, especially during the first six months, women profit from the experience more than men do in all areas other than financial. Therefore, if you decide to get a divorce, your first priority must be to take every action you can to increase your earning power. You can't rely on the goodness of your man or the courts to take care of you.

If you must go through with the actual process of divorce, your second step (as you continue to improve your financial situation) should be to consult a reputable attorney. I don't have the final word on how to find a good lawyer, but I suggest you follow the same procedure I recommended for finding a counselor; that is, get two or three names and outline the specifics of your situation; then *interview them as they interview you*. It does not follow that a female attorney will necessarily be the best for you.

It's relatively easy to tell your man you're getting a divorce. If he's made no significant effort to change, you merely have to summarize your attempts at change and his reluctance to work with you. Don't bother justifying your actions beyond this summary; chances are he will blame you for the divorce no matter what you say. If he has failed to listen to you during the past few months or years, he won't hear you now either.

It's much more difficult to tell the children. However, you can be assured that in most cases they already know that something is going wrong. Therefore, when you begin your last-ditch efforts, tell them that you and Dad are having troubles and you're trying to fix it. When the divorce is imminent, tell them the truth—that Mom and Dad will no longer live together. Keep your comments to a minimum. It's more important that you react to their questions and comments with simple truths. Do not condemn their father. (If the situation warrants it, you might say that Dad is having problems he's not able to solve.)

To minimize the impact of a divorce on your children, try to implement the following:

- Maintain consistency in your rules and discipline during the transition; changing the way you react to your children can increase their stress.
- Keep them in the same house if possible.
- If you can't stay in the house, keep them in the same neighborhood and school (if applicable) for the rest of the school term.
- Keep in mind that most children adjust to their parents' divorce within six to nine months.
- Keep in mind that divorce will exacerbate any problems a child might have had prior to the divorce.
- Children will take strength from you, so remember to take especially good care of yourself.
- If you have any questions, consult a reputable child psychologist.

Breaking the Sexual Bond

When a woman loves a man and commits herself to him, having sex with him usually bonds her to him. This bond will cause her to have hope for the future long after he has proven himself unworthy of such trust. It will also cause her to feel addicted to a man even though he may not want her anymore. The bonding does more than unite her to her man; in many cases it places her in servitude.

The bond I am talking about is too strong and universal to be purely emotional. Current theory suggests that it also has a biochemical component; that is, female hormones may impel a woman into this type of bonding. I expect that this is another genetic legacy of your prehistoric ancestors, who bonded to the men they slept with because they *had* to have their protection.

Many experts have interpreted this bonding as a kind of masochism—the secret desire to be punished. But I believe it's just the opposite. This bonding is evidence of a woman's inner strength. It's not a sick, twisted attribute. It's a very strong genetic force that's out of sync with our current culture. It only creates a problem if a woman wants to exercise the modern option of breaking the bond with a man whom she doesn't love or who doesn't love her.

If you face a situation where your man won't change and you've decided to end the relationship, it may be difficult to break your bond to him. If so, you'll have to learn a technique of countering the force, not destroying it.

Sensitization Program

The *sensitization program*, adapted to fit your unique circumstances, will help you break the unwanted bond. It will make you sensitive to the idea of sleeping with your man, so that when you think of having sex with him, you'll get an immediate avoidance reaction. This program will not work unless you want it to.

The technique of *aversive imagery*—projecting a negative image onto the screen in your mind's eye—will help you accomplish this sensitization. This is how it works.

Picture your man in a very uncomplimentary posture. The image needn't be one that's already occurred, only a situation that logically could happen. The more outlandish the scene, the better. Here are some examples of images that might cool your passion for him. Imagine that you're alone with him and he's about to kiss you, and . . .

   . . . you see snot dripping off his lip.
   . . . there are five large white zits on his nose.
   . . . he has worms crawling all over his body.
   . . . you see hair growing out of his ears.

Call upon your own favorite "turn-offs" in selecting an image that is so disgusting it immediately cools your passion. These images can be used to break, or at least dampen, the sexual bond.

Practice projecting the aversive image in nonpassionate moments. Then, each time you feel a need to be close to this man, stop what you're doing, close your eyes if you can, and picture the image, beginning with him about to kiss you.

The more you practice, the greater the success of this technique. Success also depends upon two other factors: a rational desire to rid yourself of an unhealthy sexual bond and a vividly disgusting image.

If you use aversive imagery consistently, the resultant sensitization will dissipate your desires for the man. If the program fails, it's likely that your desire for this man represents a more complicated situation and deserves more thorough study.

As soon as you've made the decision to end a relationship, set goals for yourself. Use the above information to guide your efforts. And most of all, don't look back and second-guess yourself. If you've followed even one-tenth of my recommendations, you've more than done your share. You can't take responsibility for a student who refuses to learn. You're not God.

18.

WHAT YOU'VE DONE FOR LOVE: A RECAP

Now that you've reached the end of this book, I expect that for many of you, the work has just begun. The initial success of the exercises and programs has convinced you that now more than ever, you have an excellent chance to teach your man how to give you what you need. This book demands a lot from you, but going through difficult times for love is nothing new, is it?

I want to give you a few words of caution. Your initial success could cause you to renew your habits of self-sacrifice. That, in itself, is not bad. As I've said before, I don't think that your self-sacrifice is indicative of masochism or any other "sickness." It's a marvelous trait, part of your genetic and cultural inheritance, which I think you should cherish—*but control*.

Reexamine the success you've had thus far and determine how much work your man has actually done. It won't do you any good to work yourself into a frazzle while your man sits idly by, entertained by your superhuman efforts but privately dismissing them as just more meaningless pop psychology.

When you're tempted to do all the work, remind yourself that your man is the one who must learn how to share his feelings, actively participate in resolving relationship problems, and become sensitive to your needs. You're the teacher, *he's the student.* Post this reminder on your mirror if you must.

Loving You Can Save His Life

If your man loves you and you behave as a selfless woman, he may have no reason to control his ego, learn empathy, and thereby avoid the perils of excessive self-involvement. If he indulges his every whim and you go along with it, saying nothing and swallowing your bitterness, he will definitely become selfish and spoiled. When he doesn't get his way, he'll get mad. His self-involved life style will eventually pull him into a whirlwind of hostility and insecurity.

Research in psychosomatic medicine is now beginning to confirm what common sense has suggested all along: that love can prolong life, especially in men. A twenty-five-year study of 255 physicians concluded that hostile men are six times more likely to suffer coronary heart disease than nonhostile men. In fact, hostility is closely related to most causes of death.

If your man is aware of recent reports on stress, he should know by now that it's not stress that kills but the inability to handle it. What he may not know is that "handling it" means to quit thinking of himself all the time and start truly caring about someone else. Excessive self-involvement is sending thousands, if not millions, of men to an early grave. It's within their power to stop this senseless death. All they have to do is learn to get outside themselves and love.

Psychology Can Really Help

Every since Dr. Freud came to the United States in the early 1900s to lecture about the unconscious, dream analysis, and other aspects of psychoanalysis, American psychology has been shrouded in secrecy and mysticism. "You're not going to analyze me, are you?" has been the nervous remark of countless people who believe that psychologists and psychiatrists have the power to read minds.

Since the mid to late seventies, psychology has shed its mysteriousness and become a mature science. Cognitive theory, which says that our feelings and behavior depend upon what we think, has provided a point of convergence for many otherwise divergent sciences. Because psychology and biology can now talk to each other in a common language, they are making revolutionary discoveries together.

Neuropsychology has located the cortical areas where emotions are processed. It looks as if emotions are processed differently by women than by men. It also seems conclusive that women's brains are more adaptable than those of men.

Psychoneuroimmunology is confirming that unresolved stress results in a lowering of the body's ability to fight disease. In fact, the brain is one of the world's most complete pharmacies, capable of secreting minute amounts of countless chemicals, many of which can be released at will. We've always known that a person can think him or herself into a state of health and happiness; but now we know how.

This is the kind of innovative research that I consulted when I devised these programs and exercises for a woman to use when her man won't change. *In vivo* desensitization and projected imagery are just two of the programs that have resulted from the modernization of psychology.

In spite of my great excitement about the power of today's psychology, you should remember that the human brain is not *really* a computer. You can't throw away one faulty floppy disk, and slip another, more rational one into the appropriate slot (though the idea sure is tempting at times, isn't it?). While it's clear that you can't control your man's process of choice, I do believe that you can find new ways of presenting alternatives to him so that he might change the way he chooses to behave.

During my studies, I discovered another, possibly more powerful, trend in today's psychology. The field is making a special place for the spiritual. It's clear that human beings have a need for an answer to the question, Why are we here and where are we going? Such fields as pastoral psychology and parapsychology are now recognized as something more than metaphysical speculation.

Slow Down

In my attempt to help you get what you need from the man you love, I may have unintentionally given you the idea that you have to do everything at once. You may have been in such a hurry to bask in the warmth of his unselfish love that you hit him with two empathy exercises before breakfast, three emotional analogies during a phone call at lunch, a stimulus control at dinner, and a priority checklist when he crawled into bed. If this is you, let me remind you one last time—*slow down!*

Playing Your Cards Right

I told you early on that each of us has little control over the cards that life deals us. We only control how we choose to play them. I warned you not to try and make your man play certain cards, and not to delude yourself into believing that you have the power to redeal his cards. You can only act as a catalyst—informing, demonstrating, confronting, and otherwise altering your behavior in such a way as to encourage him to change the way he plays his cards.

The programs I've outlined require that you lay your cards on the table. If your love is to survive, your man will eventually have to follow suit. He'll probably be worried that if he puts his cards on the table, you'll stop loving him. The next chance you get, remind him not to worry about that. You've already seen the worst cards he's got and you still love him. Tell him to show you some more of his good ones. That way it'll be easier for you to like him.

I believe that most men really want to learn how to deliver themselves to the life-giving power of loving a woman. I also believe that in most cases, they resist because they don't understand. So if your teaching is successful and your man learns to love you (and I sincerely hope he *chooses* to do that), there's an excellent chance that you'll be helping him to stay alive. What a wonderful gift!

A GLOSSARY OF
RECOMMENDATIONS

Below is an alphabetical listing of the recommendations made in this book. After each definition is the primary area of application. However, most of the recommendations can help you with a variety of problems. Some recommendations have universal application and are so designated.

Active listening The simple act of not putting yourself into a conversation but only seeking clarification of what the other person is saying. *Improving communication.*

Active reminiscence Recalling the pretroubled days of a relationship through pictures and identifying activities that stimulate positive feelings. The reminiscence should lead to a recreation of those activities; for example, picnicking, going to movies, canoeing, etc. *Last-ditch effort.*

Alcohol program A seven-part program for coping with an alcoholic. It minimizes the pain for family members as it maximizes the chances that he or she will seek help. *Coping with an alcoholic.*

Anchoring Finding a positive feeling about one's partner and trying to feel it a minimum of ten times a day. The goal is to build a positive base upon which to confront other issues. *Last-ditch effort.*

Anger management A five-step program designed to teach active control of irrational anger. This recommendation is founded on new research that contradicts the common wisdom of "get it off your chest." Expressing anger seems to teach people to become more angry. *Controlling bitterness.*

Appointment Making an appointment to have fun or talk about an important issue is often the best way to begin to combat the hectic schedules that may be harming a relationship. *Improving communication.*

Assertiveness training A procedure designed to teach the open and effective expression of thoughts and feelings, whether positive or negative. It can be considered the end result of a program that includes cognitive rehearsal as well as decatastrophizing, behavioral rehearsal, role-playing, and reality testing. *Controlling bitterness.*

Automatic-thoughts exercise The daily monitoring of automatic thoughts (thoughts that come into your mind without your being aware of them) for the purpose of identification and alteration. *Self-acceptance and sex-guilt analysis.*

Aversive imagery The technique of projecting a negative image onto the screen of your mind's eye. It can sensitize you to a negative aspect of another person or situation for the purpose of developing avoidance of that person or situation. *Breaking the sexual bond.*

Balancing A form of cognitive restructuring in which you identify the limits of your responsibilities. Most often, you must balance your responsibilities or your desire to please with the awareness that another always has the freedom to behave in a manner inconsistent with your intentions. *Building your social life.*

Basic communication script A basic model of communication between two people. Involves focusing on a specific behavioral issue and giving clear information. "When you do ————, I feel ————. I wish you would ————." Or: "When you say ————, I feel ————. I propose (compromise)." Or: "When you say ————, I feel ————. I counterpropose ————." *A first step in improving communication.*

Behavioral quotient The behavioral quotient of a relationship is the number of interactions out of ten that are positive in tone. *Assessing the overall adjustment of a relationship.*

Behavioral rehearsal A kind of private role-playing in which a person practices several alternative ways of saying something. It's useful as a warm-up to role-playing and especially helpful for shy people. It's critical to talk aloud during this exercise. *Practicing a new behavior in private.*

Bibliotherapy Reading the same section of a book and then discussing individual reactions as a method of stimulating communication. *Improving communication.*

Cognitive modeling Verbally addressing your inner thoughts and frustrations to an inanimate object so that your partner can hear what's going on inside of you. *Responding to an argumentative remark.*

Cognitive rehearsal The assessment of a future situation, looking for pitfalls and possible problems and deciding how to handle each one if it occurs. *Evaluating the possible outcomes of a worrisome future event.*

Cognitive restructuring Making an active attempt to replace maladaptive thoughts with more adaptive ones. A key element is the ability to "hear" your internal speech—what you say when you talk to yourself. Could be viewed as self-directed brainwashing. *Universally applicable.*

Commitment test A ten-item test to help a person determine the level of commitment he or she has to a relationship. *Determining compatibility and assessing the level of distress in a relationship.*

Communication skills Six basic skills all persons should learn in order to insure effective communication. *Improving communication.*

Companionate activity The simple act of doing things together. Research concludes that such activities as running errands, taking a walk, and shopping, if done together, can reduce estrangement. *Increasing compatibility.*

Coping statements After using imagery to project an anxiety-provoking scene, use a coping statement—"I'm a good driver," or, "I can handle that criticism,"—as a way of desensitization.

Reduction of worry about a future event or handling guilt after a mistake.

Cue-controlled relaxation A self-directed program for reducing anxiety by breathing deeply and softly repeating one word. It's to be used whenever a person identifies tension in any part of his or her body. *Reducing anxiety.*

Decatastrophizing A cognitive restructuring exercise in which a person challenges the irrational attitude he or she holds toward an event. For example, thinking, "It's not terrible if I make a mistake." *Universally applicable.*

Denominalization A method to use in identifying a marital problem or goal of change. Each partner asks himself or herself the question, "What can he/she do to love me more?" The question is then answered in three parts: a visual part (he could look at me when I talk), an auditory part (he could say, "How was your day?"), and a kinesthetic part (he could hug me, or walk into the room I am in). *Getting him to put you ahead of his work.*

Depression program A four-part program that helps people identify and cope with depression in their partners, their children, or themselves. *All depressions, except severe ones, which call for more intensive intervention.*

Desensitization Reduction of a specific fear via progressive imagery while in a deeply relaxed state. *Learning to overcome a variety of fears.*

Ego control An exercise for coping with excessive self-involvement. Talking to a friend, lover, or coworker without using the word *I*. *Reducing excessive competitiveness and self-involvement.*

Emotional analogies A procedure for facilitating the disclosure of feelings. The phrase, "I feel like ————" is used as an introduction to an analogy. The words "internal reaction" are substituted for "feelings." *Helping him learn to share his feelings.*

Emotional quotient A highly subjective rating of the personal warmth felt toward one's partner. *Assessing the strength of a relationship.*

Emotional shaping This program combines elements of others—*empathy exercise*, *strategic withdrawal*, and *projected imagery*. The focal point is the projection of the "good angel-bad angel" image. Because of your man's culture and training, the bad angel is stronger than the good one. A woman helps "shape" the strength of the good angel. *Coping with his insensitivity.*

Empathy exercise   A simple procedure to teach sensitivity to another. Essentially, one describes how another feels. *Understanding another's needs.*

Empathy quizzes   Two five-item quizzes that permit you to evaluate empathy—one for the presence of empathy, the other for the absence thereof. *Helping him learn the definition of empathy.*

Extinction   The simple avoidance of a response another person expects in a specific situation. *A key strategy for avoiding arguments, with many other applications.*

Financial confrontation   A procedure to be used when one partner in a relationship is taking financial advantage of the other one. *Confronting mental abuse.*

Flirting   Giving personal information in a nonthreatening way to a prospective partner so that he or she is encouraged to react by sharing personal information. *Meeting new people.*

Fogging   Feigning confusion or subtly changing the subject in response to an inappropriate question coming from someone who has no right to seek confidential information about your life. *Coping with nosy people.*

Forgiveness   A process for personal growth that yields the ability to forgive a personal hurt. *Renewing trust.*

Getting in the middle   A strategy of intentionally putting oneself in the middle of a family rift for the purpose of reducing the pressure. It can add temporary relief, usually without making the original problem worse. *Handling parental interference.*

Househusband shaping   A program built on the finding that if a man begins to take care of his children, he will automatically begin to do more household chores. For the shaping to be effective, the woman must reduce her guilt. *Coping with hectic schedules.*

Imagery quiz and exercise   A quick and easy method for evaluating and improving your powers of imagery. *Universally applicable.*

In vivo desensitization   A technique that permits a person to slowly take control of a situation that usually frightens him or her and that he or she typically avoids. *Overcoming a fear in a real-life setting; for example, agoraphobia.*

Last-ditch effort   A procedure comprising six other programs, to be used after all other loving confrontations have failed. *Making one last attempt to rescue a badly distressed relationship.*

Little things mean a lot   A relationship "game" played weekly to resensitize a couple to the importance of doing little things for each other. *Increasing compatibility.*

Locus-of-control exercises   Any program that teaches a person to be inner-directed. "Internals" are generally happier than "externals" (people who believe that luck often controls their lives), and have a better ability to solve problems and profit from their mistakes.

> *I-am-something-without-a-man exercise.*   An LOC (locus-of-control) exercise calling for a woman to talk for five or ten minutes without making any reference to a man.
>
> *Department store experiment.*   An LOC exercise carried out with a clerk in a department store, teaching that you have internal control over how you behave.
>
> *Puzzle exercise.*   An LOC exercise involving working on a newspaper puzzle for the purpose of learning how to solve a problem without driving yourself to perfection.

Locus-of-control quizzes   Two five-item quizzes to help you decide whether you're an "internal" or an "external." *The LOC exercises and quizzes have many areas of application, but are especially important in coping with his temper.*

Loneliness quiz   A four-item quiz to evaluate your loneliness. If you write down examples of lonely moments and give them to your partner, he may find ways of meeting your needs. *Stopping his mental abuse.*

Loneliness factors   Loneliness is caused by one or a combination of three factors: low self-esteem, worry about rejection, and depression. Understanding what to do about each factor can increase the support you get from your man. *Stopping mental abuse.*

Loving confrontation   Most of the recommendations in this book can be considered loving confrontations. The main confrontations are simple information-giving, demonstrating desired behavior, refusing to accept disrespect, offering to compromise, and a variety of extinction responses (see above). *This is the general strategy for getting what you need from the man you love.*

211

Marriage encounter weekend A "retreat" experience where couples get together for special lectures and discussions and individualized exercises designed to reestablish good communication. Reaction from participants have been mixed. *Increasing compatibility*.

Modeling Demonstrating a behavior you'd like another person to imitate. *Universally applicable*.

Negative practice An exercise in which a person is encouraged to produce the symptoms of anxiety while not feeling anxious. *Teaches the voluntary control of symptoms and therefore encourages the person to confront the anxiety-provoking situation*.

New lovers' conflict resolution A three-step procedure new lovers can use in facing and resolving their first conflict. *Turning your first fight into a positive experience*.

Nonverbal rapprochement Increasing touching and smiling in order to evoke a similar reaction in a partner who may not realize that estrangement has developed in the relationship. *Overcoming resentment*.

Opposites attract A fairly sophisticated exercise and one of the games lovers can play. It can teach couples to get past stubbornness without threatening whatever stability has been gained. Each person takes an approach opposite to the one he or she usually takes. The one who is always critical becomes supportive; the one who is always defensive become self-critical. It must be done by both partners together or it will fail. *Increasing compatibility*.

Overt self-instruction An indispensable tool for implementing cognitive restructuring. When a person uses overt self-instruction to structure a new thought, he or she should *see* new behavior, *hear* the new attitude, and *move the body* in conformity with the new attitude. *Universally applicable*.

Passive questioning The simple act of asking questions that contain no confrontations but seek only to clarify what the other person has said. *Improving communication*.

Pleasuring A daily program in which partners focus their attention on creating immediate pleasure for each other. Saying kind words, holding hands, rubbing backs, playing soft music, and giving a sponge bath are examples of pleasuring. *Taking a break from confronting problems*.

212

Positive communication checklist A twelve-item checklist for partners to use in evaluating their verbal and nonverbal communication habits. *Permits partners to work on specific aspects of communication.*

Projected imagery Using imagination to picture oneself successfully coping with a challenge. Useful in a wide range of goals, from becoming a better putter to more confidently confronting a partner. *Especially useful for gaining confidence and confronting a macho man.*

Positive self-referencing Saying positive things aloud about oneself. *Uses include relaxation during competition and improving self-esteem during the termination of a relationship.*

Priorities checklist This checklist is used to determine the relative importance of behaviors vital to a relationship. It helps partners determine the level of justice and sharing within their relationship. *Putting love and money in their proper perspectives.*

Progressive relaxation A stress-free state characterized by lowered heart and breathing rates, slower brain waves, and an overall reduction in metabolism. Much more than taking a few minutes out of a hectic day to sit down in a chair, relaxation entails the systematic release of tension throughout your body with the ultimate purpose of gaining control over the things that are upsetting you. *Universally applicable.*

Prolonged exposure Intentionally exposing oneself to a situation that is uncomfortable—through imagery or real life—the goal being a reduction of sensitivity to that situation. One must be able to terminate the exposure if necessary. *An excellent way to deal with fear of rejection.*

Quid pro quo Literally, "this for that." A way of looking at the give and take that develops (or fails to develop) within a relationship. If used as a contract, it can be an agreed-to exchange of behaviors. Each person alters some predetermined aspect of his or her behavior in accordance with the other's wishes. *Confronting his lack of support.*

Rational anger The controlled expression of anger for the dual purpose of acknowledging a feeling and getting another's attention. *Confronting sulking, among other general uses.*

Reading aloud A companionate activity during which partners read aloud to each other from mutually interesting materials. *Improving communication and compatibility*.

Reality testing Testing a proposed solution under circumstances in which failure is inconsequential. For example, testing one's assertiveness on a check-out clerk prior to asserting oneself with a boyfriend. *Universally applicable*.

Recommending books Suggesting to a partner that he or she read a book that has been recommended to you by a reliable source or that you have found helpful. *Teaching him the importance of play*.

Relabeling A type of cognitive restructuring in which a distressing situation is put in an entirely new perspective. For example, "He must hate me because he ignored me," could be relabeled, "He ignored me because he was so anxious to impress me that he was tongue-tied." Also called reframing. *To cope with the hurt of thinking he doesn't care*.

Relationship-value analysis A critically important conjoint exercise in which each partner rates his or her attitude toward the five most important values that sustain a relationship. *Recommended for use by everyone in "divorce-proofing" their relationship*.

Role-playing A flexible exercise in which a person uses a friend to practice a difficult behavior. Can be considered a warm-up to reality testing. *Many applications in reducing anxiety and worry*.

Self-critique hierarchy A technique for breaking a stalemate of isolation and distance by embarking upon a program of self-criticism. Because of barriers and lack of trust, this program should be conducted slowly and by degrees. Permits the disclosure of increasingly sensitive information. *Helping him confront his own anger and fear*.

Self-pity control A simple exercise which graphically illustrates the self-defeating nature of self-pity. To be done privately and abandoned if not experienced as humorous. *Universally applicable*.

Self-reinforcement Giving oneself a reward in response to the successful completion of a desired behavior. *Practicing confrontation*.

Sensitization A technique used to reduce undesirable behavior by associating the behavior with negative consequences. *Useful in overcoming an addiction to a past love*.

214

Sexual reevaluation   A five-step program for carefully reevaluating one's sex life. It includes the analysis of sex guilt. *Dealing with sexual problems.*

Sexual revitalization   Guidelines for coping with such problems as lack of trust, premature ejaculation, frigidity, and impotence. Involves deemphasizing performance and focusing on nonsexual massage, fondling, and kissing. *Dealing with sexual problems.*

Spontaneity exercise   A simple game that can teach a person how to take things less seriously and have more fun. *Teaching him how to play.*

Stimulus control   A procedure for anticipating a chain of events that usually leads to an undesired result, and setting up environmental conditions that make it nearly impossible for an undesirable behavior to occur. For example, removing oneself from a situation *before* the tension begins. *Coping with his temper.*

Strategic withdrawal   The gradual cessation of an inappropriate response. *Has many applications but needs to be tailored to your individual needs.*

Systematic problem-solving   A general, five-step outline of the problem-solving process: define the problem, generate possible solutions, project the outcome, agree on the best one and how to implement it, and evaluate the actual outcome. *Universally applicable.*

Ten-second kiss rule   Couples kiss each other for ten seconds twice daily without any direct genital contact. Puts romance and excitement back into a relationship. *Universally applicable.*

Therapist-initiated letter   A letter written by a therapist to a spouse who will not attend marriage counseling. Research says that a straightforward letter has a 68% chance of inducing the spouse to attend at least one counseling session. *When your partner won't go to counseling.*

Time out   A highly effective tool for controlling any disruptive situation. To be used to avoid making a bad situation worse. *Universally applicable.*

Trust renewal   A five-step program for renewing trust within a relationship. The five parts are orientation, trust quiz, desensitization, eliminating the cause, and forgiveness. *Stopping his mental abuse.*

215

Trust quiz An eight-item quiz for evaluating the level of trust within your relationship. The first step in trust renewal.

Virtues/vices continuum A program designed to help you evaluate your attraction to your man and then explore ways of helping him overcome his vices by reemphasizing his virtues. It's built upon the notion that people choose partners who possess qualities that have a bad as well as a good side to them. The chooser finds the trait virtuous at first, only later to discover that it has a dark side. Then it becomes a vice. *Getting his emotional support.*

Working-couples' management plan Guidelines that will decrease the stress associated with a dual-career relationship.

SUGGESTED READINGS

Masters, William, Virginia Johnson, and Robert Kolodny. *Masters and Johnson on Sex and Human Loving*. Boston: Little Brown, 1982.

It would be hard to find a more comprehensive and compassionate review of all the issues of sexuality than this gem. I recommended this book in Chapter 9, Dealing with Sexual Problems, because I think that if you read a few pages everyday as homework, you'll finish with few, if any, misconceptions about this very important topic.

Lazarus, Arnold. *In the Mind's Eye*. New York: Guilford, 1984.

This is an easily understood review of imagery and its varied applications. Dr. Lazarus has made many important contributions to self-management psychology, and this effort clearly identifies him as one professional who makes sense and offers real help *now*.

Rathus, Spencer, and Jeffrey Nevid. *Behavior Therapy: Strategies for Solving Problems in Living.* New York: New American Library, 1977.

Part of your role as a teacher to your man is to be familiar with behavioral psychology. Though a bit dry and professorial, this book will help you with the details of such programs as desensitization and progressive relaxation.

Tavris, Carol. *Anger: The Misunderstood Emotion.* New York: Touchstone/Simon and Schuster, 1984.

I can not overemphasize the importance of dispelling the myth that expressing your anger is good for you. It's not. The author argues conclusively that the expression of anger without the resolution of its cause only makes people more angry. This book is a must-read for those of you who want to understand and control your anger.